Martha Washington

America's first First Lady

Illustrated by Leslie Goldstein

Martha Washington

America's first First Lady

by Jean Brown Wagoner

734

Aladdin Paperbacks

Aladdin Paperbacks
An imprint of Simon & Schuster
Children's Publishing Division
1230 Avenue of the Americas
New York, NY 10020
Copyright © 1947, 1953, 1959 by the Bobbs-Merrill Co., Inc.
All rights reserved including the right of reproduction
in whole or in part in any form.

First Aladdin Paperbacks edition, 1986
Printed in the United States of America

15   14
Library of Congress Cataloging-in-Publication Data

Wagoner, Jean Brown, 1896–
  Martha Washington, America's first First Lady.

  Reprint. Originally published: Indianapolis : N.Y. :
Bobbs-Merrill, 1947.
  Summary: A biography stressing the childhood of
America's first First Lady.
  1. Washington, Martha, 1731–1802—Juvenile
literature.   2. Washington, George, 1732–1799—Family—
Juvenile literature.   3. Presidents—United States—
Wives—Biography—Juvenile literature.   [1. Washington,
Martha, 1731–1802.   2. First ladies]   I. Goldstein,
Leslie, ill.   II. Title.   III. Title: Martha Washington,
America's 1st First Lady.
E312.19.W34W33   1986   973.4'1'0924 [B] [92]   86-10737
ISBN 0-02-042160-5

To my niece, Jennie Louise,
who was born on Martha Washington's birthday,
two centuries later

Contents

Illustrations

Books by Jean Brown Wagoner

ABIGAIL ADAMS: GIRL OF COLONIAL DAYS

JANE ADDAMS: LITTLE LAME GIRL

JESSIE FREMONT: GIRL OF CAPITOL HILL

JULIA WARD HOWE: GIRL OF OLD NEW YORK

LOUISA ALCOTT: GIRL OF OLD BOSTON

MARTHA WASHINGTON: GIRL OF OLD VIRGINIA

Martha Washington

America's first First Lady

Company!

THE DANDRIDGES had company. There was nothing unusual about that. They often had company, but this was someone special. Mr. Dandridge's sister Mary had come from England. She had sailed across the ocean to visit her brothers in Virginia. In 1738 that was a great adventure.

She had arrived late the night before, after Patsy had gone to bed. Now it was morning and Patsy sat on the front steps waiting for her English aunt to wake up. Patsy's real name was Martha, but no one called her that.

"Why does Aunt Mary sleep so late, Mother?"

"It's still early," said Mother, "and she's had a long, hard journey. Besides, she's always lived in a big city, and city people don't get up so early as farmers do."

"Why don't they?"

"They haven't so much to do in the mornings as we have."

"Why not?" persisted Patsy.

"They don't have cows or oxen, or horses, or sheep, or chickens or geese to look after."

Patsy had been born on this very plantation in New Kent County on June 21, 1731. She knew

just how much work there was to looking after the animals. She had heard her mother tell the servants what to do and had seen her show them how to do it on many occasions.

The Dandridge house was on a hill above the Pamunkey River. A flower garden covered the whole front slope, and steps led down through it to the boat landing. There the big ships were loaded with tobacco for England.

Uncle William was Colonel Dandridge, Father's older brother. His plantation was across

13

the river from Father's, so Patsy could watch for him where she sat.

"Doesn't Aunt Mary own anything?" Patsy thought anyone who didn't have a single animal must be awfully poor. "Doesn't she have even one little calf?"

"No, and that's enough questions, Patsy."

Patsy sat quite still, feeling sorry for her Aunt Mary and wondering what she could do for her. Suddenly she cried, "I know! I'll go get Mrs. Waddles, and Mrs. Downy Fluff, and Mr. Nosey, and bring them to Aunt Mary. They'll cheer her up."

"Oh, no, not now," said Mother hastily. Mrs. Waddles was a pet goose, Mrs. Downy Fluff was a hen, and Mr. Nosey was a raccoon. "Suppose you watch for your Uncle William and Aunt Unity and your cousins. They'll be coming any minute. I must talk to Mammy Tuck. You call me when you see them coming."

14

Mother sat in the wide hall near the double front doors. Mammy Tuck, followed by all the house servants, came to her there. Mammy Tuck was a large, pleasant, hard-working Negro woman. She had lived with Mother for a long time. Now she was Mother's cook and ordered all the other servants around.

Mammy Tuck usually wore two aprons and two kerchiefs, a dark-colored one over a white one. Today she wore only the white, which meant she thought the company was "quality," someone worth dressing up for.

Mammy Tuck stood beside Mother, and the other servants lined up across the hall. They did that every morning and Mother gave them their orders for the day. The other servants were Sally and Susie, Mammy's helpers, Sam the houseboy, old Henry who was the butler and Mammy's husband, and Lucy, Mammy's youngest child. Then there was Joe, who did odd jobs outside.

"The William Dandridges will be here for the day," Mother began, "so, Mammy, you'd better get another ham out of the smokehouse, and a leg of lamb besides the pot roast. Have Joe catch about four hens for you. Don't be stingy with the green vegetables. Beets would be good, too, now that the weather has turned warm. Do you think of anything else we should have?"

"What kind of pies does Mrs. Mary like?" asked Mammy, looking out the front door at Patsy. "Gooseberry, maybe?"

"Oh, I'm sure she does," said Patsy. Gooseberry was her own favorite.

Mother went on giving orders. "Sally and Susie," she said, "I noticed flies in the dining room last night. Drive them out after breakfast, then close the room up tight till dinnertime."

"Yes'm," said Sally and Susie.

"See that the table linen is fresh for breakfast, but don't use the best until dinner. Get out the long banquet cloth with the thistle pattern. Use the silver on the table, not the pewter."

"Yes'm," they said.

"Henry, see that the silver is polished after each meal. And, Susie, don't bring the milk from the springhouse till the last minute, so that it will be cold."

"Yes'm."

"Sam, be ready to carry any bundles Mrs. William Dandridge may have. See that the porches are swept. Wipe up the floors again during the day if they need it."

"Yes'm," said Sam.

Right now there wasn't a speck of dirt or dust anywhere in the house. Sam had polished the floors till they were like glass.

"Now, Lucy, we're down to you. You help drive the flies out of the dining room. Get fresh green branches and wave them over the tables while we eat so the flies can't settle."

"Yes'm," said Lucy.

"Mammy, perhaps you'd better get Joe to come help. I don't think Lucy can manage both tables."

"Here they come!" shouted Patsy. "I see the boats starting across the river."

She ran down the steps and sat on the sundial in the middle of the flower garden where she could see better.

"Is that little girl my niece?" asked Aunt Mary, who came down the stairs at that moment.

"Yes, that's Patsy," said Mother.

"Patsy? I thought her name was Martha."

"It is, but that's such a grown-up name for a little girl that we nicknamed her Patsy."

"I don't approve of nicknames. Why, think of it! She may be called Patsy all the rest of her life. What kind of name is that for a fine old family like the Dandridges!"

"We thought it suited her exactly," said Mother.

"But it doesn't suit," said Aunt Mary, stiffly. "Whoever heard of anyone who was anybody being called Patsy?"

"Names aren't so important in this new country, Mary," said Mother. "There's another reason for calling our Martha Patsy. She has three cousins named Martha. One of them lives just across the river. We were always getting them mixed up."

"I do hope you aren't mistaken," said Aunt Mary.

Just then the boats bringing Uncle William and his family drew near the shore. Patsy ran down through the garden gate to meet them. Her little brothers—John, who was five, and William and Bart, aged four and two—saw them at the same time. They raced from the barn to get there first. They shoved and pushed one another to be in front on the boat landing.

"Dear me!" cried Aunt Mary. "Martha's a little tomboy, isn't she?"

Mother saw Patsy shoving and pushing, too. "Lucy!" she called. Lucy came running. "Tell Patsy to come here."

Lucy was back with Patsy in no time.

"This is your Aunt Mary, Patsy," said Mother.

Patsy smiled and curtsied. Aunt Mary was pleased. "My little niece has some manners after all," she thought.

"Patsy," said Mother, "you know better than to be so rowdy with your brothers. You are nearly seven years old now and the young lady of the house. I count on you to set the example for the boys. You're older than they are."

Patsy hung her head.

"Please don't forget again. Now," said Mother, changing the subject, "you may walk ahead of us down to the boat landing. Let your Aunt Mary see that you can act like a lady."

Lucy ran ahead and opened the gate. Patsy came next, moving like a princess, with her head high and her skirts brushing the buttercups on the edge of the walk. Mother and Aunt Mary followed slowly. They made a little procession going to meet the others.

What a lot of people were at the landing by this time! Father had seen the William Dandridges coming, too, and rode in on his horse from the tobacco fields.

Patsy's brothers were there, and Uncle William and Aunt Unity and their children. Their children's names were Martha, Elizabeth, Mary, Anna, William, and Nathaniel. They were all older than Patsy and her brothers.

Mother and Aunt Mary went to meet the newcomers.

No sooner had they landed than they saw Old Henry coming down the hill.

"There's Henry calling us," said Mother, and they all went up the hill to breakfast together.

Aunt Mary
and the Indian

THE DINING ROOM in the Dandridge house was
in the basement. There were outside steps that
led down to it, and there was also a wide stairway that led to it from the hall inside. It was the
largest room in the house and was called the
banquet hall. The walls were of red brick, and
heavy oak beams crisscrossed the ceiling. There
was a great big fireplace at each end of the room.
It was always warm in the winter and cool in the
summer.

It had a plain clay floor that was as smooth and
hard as cement. The more it was walked on the
smoother it became, except where the children

sat at the table. Their feet had gouged out hollows. When the bench they sat on was set in the hollows, it was like a seesaw. It teetered in the middle.

"It's the queerest thing," said Susie more than once, "but no matter how I set the table, the children's bench is always uneven. It just seems to move onto the hump by itself."

Mammy Tuck didn't let on that the boys shoved it there. At least once during the meal they had to jump up quickly for some reason or other. Then—zip!—everybody on the other end spilled off onto the floor. It worked every time. But of course they didn't do that when there was company.

This morning everyone went into the dining room down the inside stairway. Bart and William tried to go down the outside steps, but Lucy shooed them around the other way. "Where are your company manners?" she scolded.

" 'Twouldn't do for children to get to the table first."

Breakfast was a noisy, jolly meal. Everybody sat at one table, and all talked at once.

No other meal in the day was like this. At dinner and supper the children sat at a separate table. Everyone stood at his place until Mother and Father were seated. The children didn't speak during the whole meal, not even to ask for a second helping.

There was such a hubbub at the table this morning that Aunt Mary was horrified. "What kind of household is this?" she thought.

Suddenly everyone stopped talking. An Indian stood in the doorway! Aunt Mary screamed.

No one else was frightened. They were used to Indians. The Pamunkey and Chickahominy tribes were their friends and neighbors. They kept unfriendly Indians away and drove the wild animals out of the Dandridge woods and fields.

Father and Uncle William stood up when they saw the Indian. They knew that this was a Pamunkey scout, and they knew he wouldn't come at mealtime unless he had a special message or a gift from his chief. They went out with him. The boys stood up when the men stood, and all the little girls spilled off the other end of the bench. By the time they had picked themselves up, Mother had explained to Aunt Mary about the friendly Indian tribes.

"The Pamunkey chief probably heard that you were here and sent you a present of wild turkeys or duck or fish. They are neighborly that way," said Mother.

Aunt Mary was ashamed of her fear when she heard this. The boys were a little disappointed. They had hoped something was going to happen. "Let's go play Indian, anyhow," they said. Mother excused them from the table and they ran off to play.

"I think Mary would like to see the plantation," said Mother to Aunt Unity. "She's never seen one before. First we'll show her the workshops behind the house."

All the girls went along. The kitchen was in a house by itself. It was across a brick-paved yard back of the big house. A lane went past the kitchen and led to the washhouse where the laundry was done, to the milkhouse, the smokehouse, the barns, and the coach house and henhouse. Mother was explaining about all the work that went on at each place, when they heard shouts and yells.

Patsy Gets a Pet

"WHAT's all that noise down the lane? It seems to be coming from the henhouse," said Mother.

They hurried that way. The nearer they came to the chicken yard, the louder the noise grew. Such a cackling of hens and quacking of ducks and squawking of geese arose, a person couldn't hear himself think. The air was full of feathers from flapping wings. The fowls were in a circle about something that looked like a ball of fur. Every now and then a gander would dart toward it and peck at it. A paw would strike out and feathers would fly.

"What is it?" the girls cried. No one could tell

them at first. Then Joe darted in and picked up the animal and brought it to the children. It was a tiny bear cub.

"How did it ever get into the chicken yard?" they wondered.

"When did it come?"

"Where did it come from?"

"Watch out for the mother bear! She must be close by. She'll kill us if we take her baby."

Everybody was looking at the bear cub and asking questions and shouting.

"The mother's dead," said Joe, when he could be heard. "The Pamunkey scout said they found a dead mother bear in the woods. Someone must have shot it by mistake."

Not one of the Dandridges would kill a mother bear with her cubs. The children were taking turns holding the little animal. It seemed glad to have friends.

"Look! He's been crying!" said Patsy. "Poor little fellow."

At that the little bear let out a bawl just like a scared baby.

"Oh, isn't he cute!" said William.

"What will we do with it?" Mother asked.

"Let's keep him," the children begged.

"Keep a bear cub? Bears grow too fast and are too strong," she said. "You never can really tame a bear, either."

"We can't just take him to the woods and let him starve," William said. "He's too little to feed himself. Let's keep him till he's big enough to take care of himself."

"I know!" cried Patsy happily. "We'll give him to Aunt Mary. She doesn't have anything."

In the end Mother gave in, though Aunt Mary didn't seem very happy about her new pet. The children took the cub off to feed him and fix a sleeping place for him.

After a few weeks he was Patsy's pet. She called him Blackie. He followed her wherever she went, except when she went near the chicken yard. He grew to be almost a nuisance, especially when she wanted to work in the flower garden.

Nobody could make things grow as Patsy could. She would dig up wild flowers and plant them along the walks. People would say, "Oh, they won't grow there. You can't move wild flowers." But every time they grew.

When she was busy digging and planting, the

bear would be in the way. He would step on a new plant and crush it, or lie down on a row of tulips in a most provoking way. He was soon too big for Patsy to push away. She tied him to a stake in the ground, but it pulled loose. She tried to hide from him, but he would snuff around till he found her.

Mother worried as Blackie grew bigger and stronger, but he seemed to love Patsy and was quite gentle. That is, he was gentle with people. He got very angry at some things, like the bee martin pole.

Blackie Causes Trouble

NEARLY every plantation house had a tall pole in the yard with a birdhouse on top of it. This was for the bee martins, a very special kind of bird. They were the only birds anybody had heard of that would fight chicken hawks. Plantation folk hated chicken hawks because they would swoop over a chicken yard and make off with a baby chick or a young hen before anybody could do a thing. All other birds hid from the chicken hawk, but the little bee martin would fly right out after him to fight.

Patsy had often watched the little bee martins drive off fierce old chicken hawks. She liked them because they were so fearless. One day she saw Blackie bump into the pole and bang his nose against it. That made him angry. He stood on his hind feet and shook the pole with all his might.

"Here, here!" Patsy scolded. "What do you think you're up to?"

The bear didn't pay any attention to her. He shook the pole again. Then he dropped down and pushed with his hind end. Then he butted it with his shoulder, until he shook the house off the top. Down the house crashed!

The bee martins circled around and around it. They were frantic about the eggs that rolled out of the nests onto the ground. Patsy was as unhappy as the birds were.

"Sam!" she cried. "Come quick! Get a ladder. Hurry!" She began to put the nests and the eggs back into the house.

"Miss Patsy, that won't do any good. No bird

will set on an egg a human hand has touched. They won't use those nests again."

"Let's try it. The eggs are still warm. Please put the house back, Sam!"

Sam was sure it would not do any good, but he climbed up and put the house back on the pole. The bee martins were sitting in the trees all around. The minute Sam got the house fastened on, they flew back in.

"Hear them talking it over?" asked Patsy. "Some of them are saying everything's ruined and some are saying maybe not."

"They'll all be gone by morning," said Sam, shaking his head sadly. "And they won't come back. Any time you hurt a bird like that it warns all the rest to stay away." Sam looked as if he'd like to shoot Blackie.

"Don't you ever do that again," said Patsy to her pet. She slapped him lightly on the tender tip of his nose. He howled and howled. "Now you can just march into the house and sit there the whole time I am embroidering."

She took Blackie by one ear and pulled him into the house just as if he were a bad boy. It frightened Sam to see her. He was afraid the bear might turn on Patsy and hurt her.

Patsy sat down and picked up her sampler. She began to sew with bright-colored threads. Her finished sampler would show that she knew how to make different kinds of stitches.

The bear stretched out beside her. "Now stay there!" she ordered, and he stayed.

Blackie never touched the pole again. And Sam was wrong. The bee martins stayed.

After his mischief with the bee martins, Blackie had to snooze beside Patsy every morning from nine to eleven. He would rest his head and paws on the hem of her long skirt. She was glad to have his company while she worked on her embroidery. It gave her something to think about. With Blackie, it wasn't quite so tiresome to sew in the front room day after day.

Mother said every little girl had to learn how to sew. Patsy had to sit perfectly straight and still

40

while she did it, too. If she couldn't sit straight, a board was strapped to her back to help her. She had to sit that way for two hours, while her fingers were busy with needle and thread.

Soon she would have reading and writing lessons, too. She knew her letters and her numbers from stitching them on her sampler, but that was all. Her cousins were learning now how to act at parties and balls. They were taking dancing lessons. Even though they were older, Patsy wished they would come oftener to the Dandridge plantation. Then the hours spent in sewing would be a jolly time.

One day Mother and Aunt Mary took Patsy across the river with them to visit Aunt Unity and the cousins. All the girls went into the parlor to practice their stitches.

"I don't see how you can sit still so long, Patsy," said Cousin Elizabeth after a while. "I get so cross when we have to sew."

"So do I," said Cousin Anna. "Just look at this old thread. I could cry, it makes me so furious." She tossed the knotted and twisted embroidery silk on the floor.

"Here, I'll fix it," said Patsy.

It was fun to have someone to talk with. Sometimes, at home, Mother stopped in to help with a new stitch. But she never stayed long. Patsy picked up Anna's thread and unknotted it.

"Hand me your sampler, Anna," she said. "I'll catch up these stitches for you, if you'll show me some new jig steps."

"Oh, do mine too, please," begged Mary and Martha and Elizabeth all together.

"I'll show you how to do the minuet," promised Martha.

"I'll bring you a drink of water," said Elizabeth.

"I'll—I'll fan you while you stitch!" offered Mary.

"I can't do all of them," laughed Patsy. "Anna's having the hardest time, so I'll do hers."

Anna's sampler was a sight! It was soiled and mussed, and the stitches went every which way. Patsy's straight, neat little stitches looked out of place on it.

"Why, I can't believe my eyes or ears," cried Aunt Unity when she came in later. "You've all been here two hours, and you're still sewing."

The cousins were more surprised than their mother at how quickly the time had gone. Seeing Patsy sewing so busily and so happily had put them all in a good humor. They had forgotten to be bored! They begged Patsy to come over every day at sewing time.

When Aunt Mary looked at the girls' samplers she saw the one clean place on Anna's. "Anna," she asked, "why don't you embroider like this all the time? You should take all the rest of your stitches out and do them over. I've never seen prettier, neater, daintier work in my life."

Then Anna had to confess. "That's all Patsy's," she said.

Aunt Mary remembered how quietly Patsy worked at home—how stiff and straight she sat. "She may turn out to be a lady yet," she thought.

Everybody Goes to Williamsburg

PATSY STOOD on the window ledge by the kitchen table and watched Mammy Tuck make pies. She loved to do this and usually she was as cheerful as a cricket, but today she had nothing to say. Her face was glum.

"What's the matter, honey child?" asked Mammy. "Your lower lip's stuck out like a shelf, and your chin's pulled down on your chest. Anybody'd think you hadn't a friend in the world."

"Well, I haven't," said Patsy. "Everybody's going away. Everybody's getting new dresses. They're going to ride in a coach. They're all going to Williamsburg to see the Governor and go to parties and have fun. Everybody in the world but me!"

Mammy had to laugh. "Why, honey, I'm not going to Williamsburg!"

Williamsburg was the capital of the colony of Virginia. The Governor held his court there in the spring and fall, and people came from far and near. There were balls and dinners and horse races and theater parties.

Father went every year on business. If the children were well, Mother went along to see her friends and relatives. Mother hadn't gone for a long time, but this year Mammy Tuck had said, "You go have a rest. I'll take care of the children. I know just what to do the same as if you were here." So Mother was going. Of course Aunt Mary was going, too.

There was a lot to be done to get ready for the trip. The seamstress came to make Mother a new ball dress and make over her old gowns. The

tailor came to fit Father's clothes. His dress suits
were every bit as fancy as Mother's best dresses.
They were satin, one blue and another cream-

colored. He wore shirts with lace ruffles at the throat and cuffs, and silver buckles on his shoes. No wonder the seamstress and tailor were busy for weeks getting Mother and Father ready.

Uncle William and Aunt Unity were going, also, and they were taking their daughters. That was why Patsy felt left out. Of course her cousins couldn't think or talk of anything but Williamsburg. They were sewing ribbons on bonnets, or pinning up ruffles, or trying a new way to put up their hair, all day long. They came over to Patsy's house every day to get help from the seamstress.

"I'm getting sick and tired of it," Patsy told Mammy now, and began to cry.

Mammy's hands were full of pie dough. She wiped them off and came around the table and picked Patsy up and sat on the kitchen step with her. "Now you listen to old Mammy Tuck," she said. "Do you remember when your papa went

48

to Williamsburg the last time? Your mamma was all ready to go. She had the luggage strapped on the coach, and her pretty hat and parasol and cape all laid out. Do you remember what happened?"

"Yes. I broke out with the measles," Patsy replied.

"And what did your mother do? Did she put on that new hat and open up that parasol and throw that cape around her shoulders and strut right out of here?"

"No," said Patsy.

"Did she sit up and holler and cry all over the place?"

"No."

"No siree! She stayed at home and took care of you. Now she has another chance to go. What are you going to do about it? Are you going to set up a fuss about everybody in the world going to Williamsburg but you?" Mammy puckered up her face as if to cry. "Or are you going to smile and be cheerful like your mamma?"

"I'm going to be cheerful," said Patsy, ashamed of herself.

"Not going to let any more tears run down and make my pie dough all soggy?"

Patsy laughed out loud.

"All right, then. Get around there in your place again, and I'll make you the biggest gooseberry pie in all Virginia."

A few days after this talk Sam came in with the word that the mudholes were drying up in the woods. "The roads will be good enough for the coaches to get through to Williamsburg now," he said.

What a hurrying and scurrying there was then! Trunks were packed and loaded on the coach. Father rode all over the plantation with the overseer, giving last-minute orders. Mother was telling Mammy forty things to do at once.

50

The coaches were at the door. Everything had been loaded into them the night before.

Mother and Father were waiting for the William Dandridges to cross the river. When they finally came up the hill, the girls were so excited about going that their feet scarcely touched the ground. Uncle William was looking forward to the trip, too. But Aunt Unity wasn't. She was dressed in the height of fashion, but she looked worried and unhappy.

"Unity, what is the trouble? Are the boys sick?" asked Mother.

"No," said Aunt Unity, "but they looked so lonely as we left that I almost feel like going back."

"Why don't you let them come over here and stay with us?" asked Patsy. "I know Mammy Tuck won't mind."

"You just leave those two boys with me. We'll get along," said Mammy Tuck heartily.

52

"Oh, I'd be so relieved," said Aunt Unity. "My housekeeper is very good, but she doesn't understand boys."

So they sent Sam to bring the boys quickly. Five boys and one girl were waving good-by when the coaches started off through the woods.

"Whoa! Stop!" cried Mammy Tuck, running after them. "We forgot to throw an old shoe after you for good luck!"

But she called too late. The drivers were cracking their whips and shouting to the horses and didn't hear her.

Quick as a flash Mammy pulled off one of her own shabby old shoes and threw it after them. It fell with a loud *plop* in the road and raised clouds of dust. When they could see it Mammy shouted with joy, "Look at that lucky shoe!"

Patsy thought it looked rather sad and down-at-the-heel, but Mammy explained, "See, it's standing up. That means it's plumb full of good luck. Now you boys get a stick and pull that shoe back here to me. Don't tip it over or you'll spill some of the luck out of it."

What a time they had getting that limp old shoe back to Mammy! How they laughed to see her hopping up and down in the roadway on one foot! When the shoe was on again she said, "Since this is an extra lucky day, we'll have another breakfast. I'll let you eat it out in the kitchen garden."

They suddenly found they were very hungry. To hurry things along, the boys helped Joe drag up benches, and Patsy spread the cloth and filled the sugar bowl. Somehow or other in all the excitement they didn't remember that their fathers and mothers had gone away and left them. They were too busy on their own vacation.

Whish! Feathers!

"Oh, DEAR, I dropped my spoon again," said Patsy at breakfast.

"That's a sign of bad luck," said Cousin William. "Better throw some salt over your left shoulder."

"What good does that do?" asked Patsy.

"That breaks the spell. It keeps the bad luck away."

"Oh, that's silly. I don't believe it," laughed Patsy. Just then Mammy Tuck came in. "William says it's bad luck to drop a spoon, Mammy."

"William's right. Dropping a spoon means a disappointment before night," said Mammy, wagging her head. "Never knew that sign to fail. Throw some salt quickly."

"I don't believe it," said Patsy. But she threw some salt over her shoulder anyway.

"This is a fine day for plucking geese, Miss Patsy," said Mammy. She was talking over the day's plans just as if Patsy were mistress of the house. "There's enough wind to air the down bags, too, and it's nice and dry."

"All right," said Patsy. She wasn't paying much attention to what Mammy was saying.

"Then let's get started," said Mammy, full of vim. "You boys, we'll need your help."

This pleased the boys. It was fun to work under Mammy's orders.

"First of all," Mammy began, "we have to pen up the geese."

Mammy led the way to the barnyard, and the children followed at her heels. Just inside the gate, Mammy told them what to do.

"Make a half circle at this end," she said. "Then we'll walk toward the henhouse, shooing the geese and chickens in front of us. Don't go too fast, or you'll scare them."

The children took their places, and the shooing began. The fowls didn't suspect anything at first, but soon they seemed to notice they were being crowded together. They started running wildly, trying to find a way out. The more they ran, the more excited they became.

The children dashed here and there, trying to keep the fowls inside the tightening circle. They forgot all about going slowly.

"Slow down, everybody," said Mammy. "The hens think we're trying to catch them and put them in the pot for dinner."

They waited a little, and then began to move forward again. A big old goose flew right over Bart's head and scared him so much he wanted to leave the barnyard. Mammy couldn't let him,

though, because if he opened the gate, out would go all the geese and chickens. So Bart stayed behind Mammy. It didn't take them very long to get all the hens and geese penned up, except the one that had flown over Bart.

"Now we go to the attic," said Mammy. They went to the house and climbed to the attic.

A lot of funny bags full of feathers hung from the rafters. Mammy pointed at them and said, "The bags with blue strings have goose down in them. The ones with white strings have chicken feathers." She handed a bag to each child. "Hold on tight to these," she said. She gave a big bag with a pink string to Patsy. "This is yours," she said. "All the down off Mrs. Waddles goes into this. Don't untie the strings or we'll lose a lot of feathers. It takes years to get this many."

"What do you do with them?" asked John.

"Make feather beds, of course," said Cousin William. "I've seen the women fill a mattress tick with them at home."

"How do you get the feathers off the geese and the chickens? Isn't it hard to do?"

"We'll let Henry and Joe do the plucking. You'll see," said Mammy.

They all hurried down to the barn lot. Mammy stretched a line across the lane where there was a good breeze. Then she tied the bags on the line. "Feathers need airing every now and then," she told Patsy. "Remember that when you're saving feathers for your little girl some day."

"Are these for me?" asked Patsy.

"Most of 'em. Your mamma's been saving feathers for you ever since you were born."

"Which bags are mine?" asked William.

"Boys don't get any," said Mammy.

"Well, I'd like to know why not," said Cousin Nathaniel hotly. "I like to sleep on a feather mattress as well as anybody."

"The bride always furnishes the feather beds," said Mammy. "It's a mighty poor bride that doesn't have at least one big feather bed."

"I don't like feathers," said Bart. He was still worrying about the goose.

"Feather beds feel mighty good in the winter, though—so nice and warm," the others said.

Henry and Joe were already plucking the

geese. They worked so fast it was hard to see how they did it. They would pick up a goose and then set it down, and their hands would be full of downy feathers. They would push those feathers down into a bag with a blue string and pick up another goose.

The geese flapped their wings and waddled off as if to say, "Such stuff and nonsense!"

When Henry and Joe plucked the chickens they flapped their wings and seemed to say, "Look, look, look out what you're doing!"

When they were all plucked Mammy tied the bags carefully and let them swing in the breeze on the line. "That makes the feathers fluff up nice and fresh," she said, much pleased with the morning's work. "Now, Miss Patsy, you'd better get caught up with that sewing."

Patsy started into the house. Then she thought of the bear. She hadn't seen him all morning. "It will seem queer to sew without the silly little cub asleep on my dress. Have you seen Blackie?" she asked the boys.

No, none of them had seen him.

"Maybe he's mad at you for staying in the barnyard," said Cousin William. "He's probably found a cool place and is waiting for you."

Patsy went in and took up her embroidery and started to work. All at once there was such a screeching down the lane that she dropped her sewing basket and ran to see what had happened.

"Look at that bear! Stop him! Stop him!"

Sally and Susie were wringing their hands. Blackie was standing on his hind legs, and he was swatting the feather bags playfully. Each time he swung, his claws ripped open a bag. The wind caught the feathers and scattered them everywhere. It looked like a January snowstorm in the lane.

"Oh, oh!" cried Patsy. "There go Mrs. Waddles' feathers!"

She was so upset she snatched up a stick and whacked Blackie right on the end of his nose. The bear howled, and then ran off down the lane. He stopped once and rubbed his nose. He looked at Patsy as if to say, "I don't like you any more."

Patsy called, "I don't like you, either."

Blackie lumbered off toward the woods.

Mammy stood looking at the torn bags and the few feathers left. "I knew we were due for trouble when Miss Patsy dropped that spoon."

Patsy still thought the spoon had nothing to do with it, as of course it didn't. "Mother said we really couldn't tame a bear. Blackie was just getting even with the geese that pecked him when he was little."

That was the last Patsy ever saw of Blackie.

She felt sad about him when she got over being angry. The boys went out and looked for him every day, but he had gone off with his own kind.

Where Is Patsy?

"Somebody's coming today. My nose itches and that's a sure sign," said Mammy Tuck one morning.

The children were all eating breakfast in the kitchen. Mammy allowed it this one time because Sally and Susie were cleaning and polishing everything in the dining room.

"Maybe Father and Mother will get home," said John.

"No, this is company."

"They're bringing the company," said Bart. He was awfully homesick for his mother.

The children stayed close to the house all

morning, waiting. It was tiresome and they began to get cross.

"Let's play hide-and-seek," said Patsy.

"We might get too far away just when they
come," said Cousin William.

"We'll make it a rule that we have to hide in
the house."

"The hall table is base and the last one there
is 'it.'"

Everybody raced for the hall table. Of course
little Bart was last.

"That won't be any fun," said Cousin Nathaniel. "Bart can't find anyone."

"All right, one person will hide and the rest
will seek," said Patsy. "That way Bart can play
just as well as the rest of us."

The children took turns hiding, and the game
was as much fun as regular hide-and-seek.

Finally it was Patsy's turn. She knew exactly
where she was going to hide—in the bottom of

the cupboard in the dining room. She slipped down the stairs as quietly as a mouse. The steps didn't squeak once.

When she reached the dining room door, she stopped and looked back. No one was watching her, so she started across the room toward the

big cupboard. Then she saw something that made her eyes fairly pop.

At the far end of the dining room there were big heavy doors, one on each side of the fireplace. They were always locked. One door was bolted, also. Patsy had never seen these doors open. She had no idea what was behind them. Father had told the children they were not to open them.

Today, this very minute, that heavy, bolted door was standing wide open! Patsy ran to it and tried to see in. It looked like a big black cave. She and her cousins had pretended her father kept pirates or wild animals in there. But she couldn't see a thing.

Just then she heard the boys coming to find her. "I'll just step inside the door," she thought. "I won't go all the way in, and I'll pull the door nearly shut so that they won't notice it. They'll never think to look for me here."

She was so pleased to think she had found such a good place that she skipped behind the door, pulled it to—and then something happened. A gust of wind pushed the door shut and the latch fell in place with a click. Patsy was locked in!

Sally came into the room at that moment and saw the boys coming down the stairs. "Now you children get right out of this room. We just finished cleaning it and I don't want one little bit of it mussed up."

Right at that very second they all heard another sound: horses' hoofbeats coming at a gallop out of the woods.

"Hurrah! Hurrah! They're here! Come on, Patsy!"

But Patsy didn't hear them. The heavy door shut out all sounds.

The other children ran out pell-mell. Little Bart fairly went head over heels in his hurry.

There was much shouting and hugging and kissing for a little bit. Mother thought maybe she couldn't see Patsy because there were so many people in the way. She kept looking for her. So did Father. Finally they were sure that she wasn't there.

"Where's Patsy?" they asked.

"Why, she was right here," all the boys said.

Then William remembered. "She's hiding."

Mother thought that was rather queer.

"We were playing hide-and-seek when you came," they explained.

John ran to the door and shouted into the house, "Patsy! Come on out! The game's over. Father and Mother are here."

Still there was no Patsy. How quiet it seemed all at once. Father shouted as loudly as he could, then listened. It seemed as if the whole plantation and the meadows and woods listened for her answer. There wasn't any.

"She has to be right here," the boys insisted. "She must be teasing us."

"Where were you playing?" asked Father.

They told him exactly where they had been. They went into the house and called and called.

"Maybe she hid outdoors," said Uncle William.

"No, we ruled you had to hide in the house. Patsy wouldn't cheat," Nathaniel said.

"Then she's in the house, but we can't hear her. So she is either hurt or in a deep closet."

When Aunt Mary heard that, she fainted dead away. The girls began to cry. Mother and Father thought right away of the dining-room closets. They ran down there as fast as they could go.

The Gun Room

BEHIND the big door Patsy stood quite still. She thought, "If there are pirates or animals in here, I'll hear them moving around." She didn't hear a thing. She was certainly glad she didn't.

"If I walk or feel around in here I might get my dress dusty. I want to look nice when Father and Mother get here. If I sit down I'll get mussed, so I'll just stand right here at the door. They'll find me in a minute."

After a minute she said, "It's awfully dark. I wonder how long I've been in here. I'd lie down and take a nap, but I'd be sure to get dirty *and* mussed then. It must be suppertime by now."

Then the door flew open and there were Father and Mother, and it was still bright daylight. Patsy couldn't believe her eyes. How they all laughed when she told them what she had thought! Patsy laughed, too.

Father was glad when he learned that Patsy hadn't opened the door. He would have been sorry to punish her the first minute he came home.

"How did the door happen to be open?" he asked.

"I opened it," said old Henry. "You told me to clean the guns while you were gone. I thought this would be a good day because Sally and Susie were polishing in here and would keep the children out of the way."

"Guns!" cried all the boys. "Is that what you keep in there?"

"Yes," said Father. "Bring a lantern, Henry, and we'll show them."

Henry brought the lantern and stepped inside the door and held the light high above his head. The children crowded around the door. They looked into a big room lined with brick. Along one wall hung powder horns. On another were guns, and on a stone shelf were bags of gunpowder.

Father pointed to the gunpowder. "That's why I kept this door locked. I didn't want any children near that powder. They might get blown up."

"I didn't know you had all these rifles, Uncle John," said Cousin William. "Do we have some, too, Father?"

Uncle William nodded.

"Every planter has a room something like this," said Father. "It's the gun room. In the old days every man had to be ready to fight the Indians at any instant, day or night. He had to have enough guns to arm any neighbors who

came for help. He had to have enough ammu-
nition to last a long time. Sometimes our fathers
were a whole year without fresh supplies."

"I'm glad we don't need gun rooms any more,"
said the girls.

The boys weren't so sure. "It must have been
pretty exciting in those days," they thought.

"Now, Henry, lock up the room again. Put the key in a safe place where the smaller children won't find it."

Then they all went upstairs, the grownups, the children, and all the house servants. Father and Mother opened their trunks. Tucked into the corners and in the folds of satin coats and dresses were packages of all shapes and sizes.

"Let's see now," said Father mysteriously. "What have we here?" He reached down into the middle of the trunk and pulled out a package. "I do believe this is for Master John Dandridge."

"Open it, open it!" said the others. They crowded around him.

John was so excited he nearly dropped it. When he saw what he had, he let out a shout. "A knife! A knife! Oh, thank you, Father." John began whittling at once.

Already Father was giving out other things.

There were marbles for William, a popgun for Bart, a humming top for each boy—but nothing for Patsy. She didn't want to be unladylike, but she could hardly keep from screaming out, "What do you have for *me?*"

"Stop your teasing now, Father," said Mother. "Show Patsy what we brought for her."

Then her father picked up the biggest bundle of all. It lay right on top of everything. The moment Patsy opened it she cried out, "Lucy! Come quick! It's for you and me!"

There were two dolls in Patsy's arms. They were the most wonderful dolls Patsy had ever seen. They were made of wood. Their faces had been painted on. They had pink cheeks and big blue eyes. Of course their eyes didn't open and shut, and they didn't have any hair, but Mother had dressed them with scraps from her own gowns.

Lucy could hardly believe her eyes when she

saw the dolls. When Patsy gave her one of them, she danced a jig right then and there.

Every house servant was given a present, earrings or bright kerchiefs to wear on Sundays, or a new shirt. After supper the field hands came up to the house and every one of them got something, too—a present from Williamsburg.

"It's almost as good as Christmas!" they all said.

A Man Comes
to Paint a Picture

ANY TIME in the day when the children were out of sight, Mrs. Dandridge was pretty sure where they were. No one needed to tell her. There was just one place where they would be. That was the race track.

Every plantation had its own oval dirt track where the horses were trained. Some horses were trained for racing, and some for the saddle. Some were trained to be used only for the coach.

The Dandridge track was in the meadow below the barn. The children never tired of watching Mr. Smith, the trainer. He taught them all to ride, too.

The three boys had their own ponies, even little Bart, who had just had his third birthday. Patsy had a saddle and a riding habit, but no pony. "You're too little to ride yet," Mr. Smith said.

"But I'm the oldest," said Patsy, "and I'm much taller than Bart. Look!" She stood back to back to Bart, to show Mr. Smith that she was more than a full head taller.

"Ladies ride sidesaddle, though," Mr. Smith reminded her kindly. "You have to be taller to ride gracefully. You don't want to look like a country bumpkin."

No, Patsy decided, she didn't want to look like that. When she was tall enough to ride, she would do it properly and gracefully.

Mr. Smith cut a long slit in the gatepost. "When you reach this mark, it will be time for you to learn to ride," he said.

So, day after day, Patsy sat on the fence and

watched her brothers ride. Day after day she listened to Mr. Smith as he gave the boys their lessons. She learned many things about riding from watching and listening.

There came to be a column of little nicks on the gatepost. They were the marks Mr. Smith made from time to time when he measured her height. Patsy always wanted to stand on her toes when she was being measured, but she didn't. The little nicks were creeping toward the big mark, anyway.

Then came the big moment in John's life. Mr. Smith was going to let him jump his pony for the first time. He was going to race one of the cousins' ponies. The children were all down at the track to watch.

John's cheeks were red with excitement. His eyes danced. The boys rode their ponies to the starting post. Mr. Smith stood ready to give the signal when there came a shout.

Everyone looked up. Sam came running to
the gate. He had a message from "Old Miss,"
as all the servants called Mother.

"Old Miss wants the children up to the house.
The picture man is on his way and she wants
them to get dressed up. She says to hurry all of
them up there right this minute."

Poor John! He was so disappointed he just wilted off his pony. "I knew this was too good to be true," he said. He handed the pony's reins over to Mr. Smith. When Mother sent word for the children to come, they came.

On the way to the house they noticed how hot and sultry the day was. It had seemed quite pleasant in the meadow.

"It's too hot to dress up," said John.

The others agreed, but they took care not to say it where Mother would hear them. She guessed their thoughts when she saw their long faces as they came into the house.

"I know it's hot," she said, "but a storm is coming up. That will cool things off soon. In the meantime put on your Sunday clothes. Aunt Unity is on the way over with Mr. Lyttle, and I don't want to keep him waiting."

Mr. Lyttle was an artist who had come from Williamsburg. He was going to begin a painting of all the children—Patsy, John, William, and Bart. Mother and Aunt Unity had met him while they were away, and had seen some of his pictures. "We really must have him come and paint pictures of our children," they had said.

The boys and girls liked the idea, too. When they learned they had to dress up, though, the boys changed their minds.

"John," said Mother as the children went to dress, "your father and I decided that you should wear your new clothes for this picture."

John brightened up at this news. Things weren't so bad as they had seemed a minute ago. His new clothes meant his first breeches.

Like the other boys, he had worn dresses until he was six years old. The boys didn't call them dresses, even though the clothes looked like them. They were long coats, that touched the floor all the way around. Underneath the coat they wore long petticoats.

Today Bart and William wore stiff dark blue satin coats and embroidered satin cream-colored petticoats. They were beautiful, but very hot.

John's suit was of fine green wool trimmed with fancy buttons. His knee breeches were fastened with silver buckles, and he wore silver buckles on his shoes.

"This high collar is choking me to death," he said, but he was secretly proud of his new finery. He strolled over to the mirror as if to look at a speck on his nose. It was really to get a peek at himself. He was dressed exactly like his father. Even the lace ruffles of his shirt sleeves rippled like his father's when he raised his arm.

"He's the very image of his father," said Aunt Mary.

John was so pleased he didn't complain much even when they brought out the wig.

"Your father always wears one to church," said Mother.

"But his isn't a curly one like this."

"This is much more stylish," said Aunt Mary, and that was the end of it.

Mammy Tuck and Henry and Sally and Susie and Sam all helped get the boys dressed. Patsy was ready a long time before they were. Lucy helped her.

While the others were still worrying with buttons and buckles, Patsy was practicing walking in her new high-heeled satin slippers. Now that she was past eight, she would wear high-heeled slippers whenever she dressed up.

She walked up and down the cool hall and pretended that she was a queen. Every now and then she whirled so that she could see her cape sweep the floor. She liked the feel of her silk dress, too. The long silk skirt felt much nicer than her everyday linen and cotton ones.

Long before they were all ready, Aunt Unity came with Mr. Lyttle. The girl cousins came,

too. They had heard that John was to wear his first suit. Sam was sent to let Father know when John was ready.

When Father came in he carried a small silver sword. The scabbard was engraved with the family coat of arms. The blade flashed, it was so bright. "This belongs to you, now," he said, and held it out to John. "My father gave it to me the day I wore my first suit."

John couldn't take his eyes off it. He couldn't even speak except to say, "Thank you, sir."

By the time everyone was through admiring John and the shining sword, it was close to dinnertime. The sun had gone under a cloud. It grew darker and darker in the room. Henry rang the dinner bell.

"Perhaps it will clear away after dinner," Mother said.

They all went down to the dining room. The children stood at their places until the grownups were seated. They meant to sit down, too, but several things happened. John couldn't see over his collar and missed the bench and sat on the floor instead. William's and Bart's coats were so stiff and slick they wouldn't bend in the middle so they had to remain standing. Patsy sat down on the bench all right, but slid right off because there wasn't anyone to hold down the other end.

So they all decided to eat their dinner standing up.

"If we don't, we'll be too mussed to be in the picture. That would be too bad after all the trouble we've had getting ready," said Patsy.

Patsy Tries
to Please

"It's STILL too dark to begin painting," the artist said after dinner, "but we can decide several things. How big do you want the picture? What shall each child be doing in it? Shall they sit or stand? I shall also show you what each one will be holding."

"Do we have to hold something?" asked Bart.

"Yes, indeed," said Mr. Lyttle. "My pictures are famous for the fine things the children hold in their hands."

"I'd like to hold my sword," said John.

"No, it would take too long to paint that," said Mr. Lyttle. "The things I have brought with me will do very well and I can paint them almost with my eyes shut."

He told Sam to bring him the bag he had left in the hall. The boys crowded around to see what was in it.

At first Bart thought Mr. Lyttle had brought his lunch with him. Then suddenly he began to howl, "Take it away! Take it away!"

Mr. Lyttle had handed him a stuffed owl. "Don't you like it?" he asked in astonishment.

Bart threw the owl to the floor. He didn't like the feel of its claws on his hand.

"Be careful," cried Mr. Lyttle, "you'll spoil it."

"Take it away," yelled Bart again.

His mother tried to quiet him. "It's not a live bird," she said. She picked it up and stroked it. "See, it's pretty. It's a stuffed owl."

"I don't care. I don't like it," said Bart.

"Maybe he'd like a blue jay," suggested Mr. Lyttle. He handed one to Bart. Bart threw that on the floor, too. Mr. Lyttle looked very unhappy. "All the other children have been very fond of the stuffed birds," he said.

"Does he have to hold a bird?" asked Patsy. She saw an apple in the satchel. "Why can't he hold the apple?" she said.

"No, no," said Mr. Lyttle. "Babies hold those. Boys are always supposed to hold birds."

"Dear me," said Aunt Unity, "I had no idea it would make any difference about what they held. I'm sure Bart wouldn't want people to think he was a baby, though."

"Of course not. Would you, Bart?"

"I don't care," said Bart. "I hate those things." He shoved the birds away with his foot.

Mr. Lyttle looked as if he would like to pick Bart up and spank him right then and there.

Patsy knew how Bart felt. "Bart has a little pet turtle," she said. "Couldn't he hold that? It won't be hard to paint."

Mr. Lyttle nodded. "That might be the very thing," he said. "Will someone get the turtle for us right away?"

Lucy was sent out to bring the turtle from the tool shed where they kept it. Bart joyfully took it, and did just as the artist told him to and didn't make any more trouble.

"Now, the next boy should hold a dove," Mr. Lyttle said. He handed William a white bird. "Hold it on your finger. Now act as if you were going to let the little dove fly away," said Mr. Lyttle.

"Oh, that's silly," said William.

"William," said Mother, "we're not going to argue with you. Bart was too little to know any better, but you can do as you're told."

"But, look," said William. "Who ever saw a boy as big as I am playing with a dove?"

Everybody looked crossly at William. "Oh, dear," thought Patsy, "if he says another word he'll be punished." Then she said to her mother, "William likes the globe Father has. Couldn't he hold that?"

Mr. Lyttle looked relieved. "That would be quite all right," he said. "One of my best pictures was made with a globe in it."

So Lucy ran and brought Mr. Dandridge's globe of the world, and everybody was happy again.

"Now," said Mr. Lyttle, "the oldest boy will

hold this." He proudly brought out a stuffed eagle.

John didn't look proud or pleased. He looked disgusted. "Look!" he begged. "I don't see why I have to carry a smelly old bird when I have a fine silver sword."

Everybody began to scold John at once.

"This is enough to try the patience of a saint," said Aunt Mary. "It would serve you right to give you the apple to hold."

"It must be the weather," said Mother. "I've never known the children to act this way before. Really, John, I had counted on you to set a good example."

"Can't you think of something?" Mammy whispered to Patsy. "Your mamma's going to send for the Old Man if this keeps up." All the servants called the master of the house the "Old Man."

Patsy was as unhappy as John was. She knew

how she would feel if the sword were hers. So she thought very hard.

"If John held his sword so only the handle showed," she said, "would it take too long to paint?"

Mr. Lyttle wasn't sure. Everyone else liked this idea. Even Aunt Mary said if Mr. Lyttle couldn't paint a handle as quickly as a whole bird, he wasn't so fine an artist as they had thought.

"Very well," he agreed, "let us try it. We'll see how it looks."

John stood as straight as he could with the sword at his side and his hand on the hilt.

"Oh, that's wonderful," cried Mother. "His father will be delighted." So that settled that.

At last they were ready to see what Patsy was to carry. The artist reached into the bag. He fumbled around in it. Then he carried the bag to the window, and scraped around in it. "Dear me," he cried in dismay. "I had a wreath of flowers for the young lady. It seems to be gone."

"It's still at our house," said Cousin Elizabeth. "I saw it on the table."

This time everyone had the same idea. "There are plenty of flowers in the garden. We'll use real ones," Mother said.

Everyone started toward the doors to get them. The doors were quite wide, but of course they couldn't all get through at one time. Mammy and Sally and Susie jammed in the first doorway. The cousins started out the other door and bumped heads. The boys hopped over the low window sills and dropped to the ground. Patsy was so tiny that she squeezed between Mammy Tuck and Susie and was out in the garden before anyone—and then it happened!

Crack! Boom! The lightning and thunder came almost together. Rain came down in buckets. Mother and Aunt Unity ran to the hall.

Had the house been struck by lightning, they wondered. But the house was safe. The boys and Patsy ran for the front porch.

"Patsy!" cried Mother. "Look at your slippers!"

Patsy had hurried to get in before the rain. She hadn't noticed where she stepped. Her slippers were black with the garden dirt.

This was the last straw. It seemed that the picture just wasn't to be painted that day. Then Mr. Lyttle helped Patsy. "Miss Patsy Dandridge really shouldn't wear shoes in a picture of this kind," he said. "The little ladies in the picture galleries are barefoot."

So Patsy stepped out of her satin slippers. The artist was delighted. "Miss Patsy's is the smallest, daintiest foot I have ever painted," he declared.

The storm was over soon. The sun came out. The air was cool and fresh. The artist got out his paints and brushes, and the picture was begun after all.

Mother and Aunt Unity and Aunt Mary were proud and pleased. The children were good as gold. But they all hoped it wouldn't take the artist many days to finish the picture.

Looking for
Betsy Bee

VOICES outside her window woke Patsy early
one morning. Ned was talking to Mother. Ned
was one of the stableboys who milked the cows.

"Betsy Bee is gone," Ned was saying. "There
must be a hole in the pasture fence. Or else the
Indians drove her off."

"I don't believe the Indians took her, Ned,"
said Mother. "How long has she been missing?"

"I couldn't find her last night," he answered.

"You should have told me then," said Mother.
"Don't bother Mr. Dandridge about it. He's too
busy with the tobacco crop now. Bring me my
horse and we'll ride down to the pasture. We

may find her if she hasn't wandered off too far. At least, I hope we can find her."

"Yes, ma'am," said Ned. He ran toward the stable.

"May I go with you?" Patsy called out the window.

"Yes," said Mother. "Get your bonnet and mittens. We may go for a long ride. The sun will be high before we're back."

Mrs. Dandridge was always careful about bonnets and gloves. She didn't want her complexion or Patsy's spoiled by freckles, sunburn, or tan.

By the time Ned was back Patsy was ready. He lifted her up on the horse in front of her mother. He rode one of the old field horses. They started off down the lane past the washhouse, the milkhouse, the barn, and coach house, through the cow lane to the fields.

While they rode Patsy thought about her one

big wish. "Do you think I can have a pony of my own someday?" she asked.

"Yes, and it won't be very long," said Mother. "Your father has sent for one."

Patsy couldn't believe her ears. "Did you say Father had sent for one for me?"

"Yes, Patsy."

"I was hoping that's what you said. Will it come on this ship?" she asked hopefully.

"It's been due a long time," said Mother. "Your father is beginning to be worried."

"Is he afraid the ship s-s-sank?" Patsy was so anxious she stuttered.

"No, because it's a good stout ship. It's one of your Uncle William's. Father is afraid the winds may have blown it off its course."

"Is that very bad?" asked Patsy.

"It just takes the ship much longer to get here. The sailors run out of food and water and have to stop at some other port. That takes more time.

Then the seed spoils. Rats and mice get into it and they gnaw holes in everything, the woolen cloth, the flower bulbs and——"

"What happens to my pony?"

"Your pony is probably tired of the ship by this time. You must let it roll over and over in the grass when it comes."

Patsy laughed with joy. What fun it would be to see her own pony rolling in the grass!

By this time they were riding through the cornfield. Soon they came to the pasture.

"Keep a lookout for any broken place in the fence now, Patsy," said Mother. "I don't see a sign of a hole yet, do you?"

"No, but I see Betsy Bee," said Patsy.

"Where?" asked Mother in surprise.

Patsy pointed to the cow over near the river, outside the fence. Betsy Bee was caught in a tangle of wild grapevines.

"Ned," Mother called, "ride around and get

her and take her to the barn. She may have eaten poison weed or mullein. That would spoil her milk, so keep it separate for a few days."

"Yes, ma'am," said Ned. "Do you want me to find out how she got outside the fence?"

"No," said Mother. "You take care of Betsy Bee. Patsy and I will ride till we find the break."

Ned rode off. "I'm glad we found Betsy," said Mother. "I was sure the Indians didn't take her."

"Why did Ned think they did?" asked Patsy.

"Because some of our friends have all kinds of trouble with the Indians. They drive off the fine horses, burn the barns, and even burn down the houses and carry off the women and children."

"Our Pamunkey Indians wouldn't do that," said Patsy stoutly.

"No, we're lucky to have them and the Chickahominies as neighbors. Now let's see how Betsy Bee got out."

They rode along the fence. Finally they came to a big oak tree that had fallen across the fence and knocked it down.

"The lightning must have struck this tree," said Mother. "See where it is split in two? Now we must ride to the village and get Ben Moore.

He'll mend the fence so we won't lose any more cows."

"How did Betsy Bee find the broken place?" Patsy wanted to know. "It was hard to see."

"The cows often graze along the fence. When there's a hole they wander through and are soon lost."

"Why don't they come back in?"

"They don't know they're lost," laughed Mother.

"Not even when it's night?"

"No. That's why we tie bells around their necks. Every time they move the bells jingle, and we can find them even in the dark."

"Why didn't Ned hear Betsy's bell?"

"I think Ned was afraid to come down here after dark, don't you?" Mother asked.

"But Betsy might have stayed lost. What happens when a cow isn't found?"

"If she's lost in the swamp, she may drown,"

said Mother. "If she's lost in the woods, the wolves may get her."

"I don't like wolves," said Patsy. "When I hear them in the night I pull the covers up over my head."

"That's silly," said Mother. "Wolves are cowardly. They don't come near the house. They stay deep in the woods where people can't see them."

"I don't like them anyway. They killed a little lamb last year. Why don't we put bells on the lambs?"

"We put bells on the rams. The sheep always follow them. But we have to be watchful in the early spring at lambing time. The mother sheep may hide their lambs away. We have to find them before the wolves do."

"What's the matter with the sheep? Don't they have any sense? They ought to bring the lambs to the fold where we can take care of them. Why do we have to keep sheep anyway, when they cause so much trouble?"

Patsy still felt bad about the lamb. She spoke as if she hated sheep, but she really didn't. She knew that wool came from sheep. Without wool, she would have no warm winter clothes.

Patsy and her mother rode on till they came to the plantation village. All the shops were here. Everything needed on the whole plantation could be made or mended here.

The first shop that Patsy and her mother saw was a cobbler's, where a shoemaker made and repaired shoes. The next shop was a blacksmith's, where a man made horseshoes, tools, and many other things from metal.

The blacksmith was shoeing a horse when Patsy and her mother rode by, but he stopped to wave at them. Patsy waved back.

Beyond the blacksmith's, there were some more shops. There were a carpenter's shop, a tailor's, a weaver's, a tanner's—every kind of shop. The cabins of the men who worked in the fields were there, too.

Mother rode to Ben Moore's shop and told him about the broken fence.

"We'll yoke up the oxen right this minute," he said. Some Negro boys loaded good stout rails onto the oxcart and they started off for the pasture. The boys rode on the back of the cart.

"I guess the wolves won't get any of our cows for supper tonight," said Patsy.

"No, but they might have had Betsy Bee if you hadn't seen her."

"Will you punish Ned for not finding her last night?"

"No, I think not," said Mother.

"But cows are hard to get. He should have gone after her last night."

"Would you have gone, Patsy?" asked Mother.

"No, of course I wouldn't."

"Then you can't blame Ned, can you?"

Patsy was silent.

"You must learn not to be afraid," said Mother kindly. "You should not expect other people to do things you would not do yourself. Remember, a woman should always try to set a good example for her household."

"Everyone at the plantation ought to be good and brave and kind, then," said Patsy, "because that's what you are."

She thought about it all the rest of the way to the house. "I'll try very hard to be like you, too," she said.

Patsy Makes
a Wish

IT HAD been a hot day, but it was nice out on the front porch now. Supper was over. Everyone was out there. The cousins came. The Woodhouses and the Lydalls from neighboring plantations came, too. They were all singing. The girls were teaching the boys some of the songs they had learned in Williamsburg.

The sun went down. The fireflies began to twinkle in the tall grass along the river. A whippoorwill sang in the tree beside the house. Everybody was still for a minute.

"Whatever are you doing, Patsy?" Cousin Martha asked suddenly. Patsy's eyes were shut

tight and her face was screwed up as if she had
a stomach-ache.

"I was wishing on that bright star," said Patsy.
"It's the first one I've seen tonight."

"You look as if it hurt you," said Martha.

"That was because I was wishing so hard."

112

"What do you want as much as all that?" asked Cousin Elizabeth.

"Oh, she mustn't tell, or it won't come true," said Cousin Martha, "but I know what *I* wish. I wish that the ship from England would come in tomorrow."

"So do I!" shouted the others together.

Everybody wanted the ship to come.

To see a ship come was the most exciting thing that could happen to the Dandridge children. They had never been in a city. They had never seen long rows of buildings. The grown-ups had often told them about the city shops, but the city wasn't so real as the ship.

The ship brought everything they wanted right to their very own boat landing. It came only about twice a year. They were as excited about it as they were about Christmas.

"What do you want the ship to bring you, Martha?" Patsy asked.

"I want it to bring the satin for my wedding dress." Martha was going to be married.

"I want it to bring me an ivory fan set with brilliants," sighed Cousin Mary. "I saw one at the Governor's ball like that. It was lovely!"

"I don't want silly things like that," said Cousin Nathaniel. "I want a sword like John's."

That started the others off. Cousin William wanted a shuttlecock set. William wanted a gun. Bart wanted a hobbyhorse.

A horse! A pony! Patsy shut her eyes and crossed her fingers and wished.

There was one thing she wanted more than anything in the whole world, and that was a pony. Mr. Smith had said she was almost tall enough. She dreamed at night about it. She could see herself jumping on her pony's back and galloping off over the fields.

She was so busy with her own thoughts she hardly heard what the others wished, until Father said, "I want the ship to bring me some grass seed."

"Grass seed, Father!" she cried, laughing merrily. "That's nothing to wish for. There's grass everywhere already."

It did look as if Patsy were right. The slopes and meadowlands around the Dandridge plantation were covered with deep rich grass.

"The grass you see around here I sowed myself," said Father. "It never was good grass before. That down by the river and in the bottom lands is still rank. I need more seed for more pasture land."

This kind of talk didn't interest Patsy. She went back to her own dreams. Before she knew it she was asleep on the porch. Mammy Tuck carried her into the house and put her to bed. Patsy didn't even remember how she got there when she woke up the next morning.

The Ship Comes In

BOOM! BOOM! What was that? Patsy sat straight up in bed. It sounded like a cannon!

Boom! The windows rattled. The ground shook. It must be a cannon! Hurrah! There was only one cannon that she had ever heard near the plantation. That cannon was on the ship.

Patsy sprang out of bed and ran to the window. It was barely daylight. She began to make out a shape on the river. It *was* a ship. "The ship's in, the ship's in!" she cried.

From all over the house the same cry arose. Out on the lawn flares were started. The workers came running from over the fields, shouting and

cheering. The ship's coming meant a holiday for them. No one would work today or tomorrow.

They began to gather wood for a great bonfire. There would be a big barbecue. The smell of meat cooking over the open fires would fill the air. The Indians would bring wild turkeys, a wild boar maybe, or even a bear. There would be pigs roasting over the coals.

Oh, there would be lots of good food, and people would come from plantations for miles around. A ship's coming was the most fun in all the year. And in this ship there might be at this very minute a beautiful pony that belonged to Patsy Dandridge.

All these thoughts raced through Patsy's head while she tried to dress. "Where are my underclothes? Where are my petticoats? Where's my dress? Hurry, hurry, hurry."

"I'm ready at last," she cried, and started out the door. "Oh, I forgot my shoes and stockings."

118

She ran back into her room. She felt around on the floor. "Where are they?"

It was still too dark to see. Why didn't someone come to help her? Where was Lucy, anyway? What did she mean not being here when Patsy needed her?

"I'll give her a piece of my mind," Patsy scolded to herself. "Making me miss all the fun. What did she do with my slippers?"

Finally she found them. Then she found the stockings, but they were twisted. Patsy was so excited her fingers were all thumbs. She was so vexed she was almost crying, when Lucy popped in all out of breath.

"Lucy," she cried sharply, "where have you been?" Patsy was going on to say some hard things; then she stopped herself. In the nick of time she remembered. "You should try to set a good example for the household," her mother had said.

119

Lucy, in the meantime, was on her knees putting Patsy's stockings on. She had straightened them out as if by magic. Then she put the slippers on. All the time she was saying, "Oh, Miss Patsy! There's news for you. Run to your mother's room. There's something a lot more exciting than the ship right there in your mother's room!"

Patsy couldn't quite understand what Lucy was saying. Something more exciting than a ship? Lucy must have a fever or something.

"What is it, Lucy?" All at once Patsy was scared. "Isn't Mother all right? Why isn't she out seeing about the barbecue? They'll all be asking for her."

"Just go see," laughed Lucy. "You're not going to be the only girl around here any more."

Then Patsy did run as fast as she could go to her mother. Something more exciting than a ship! Patsy had a baby sister.

Who Has the
Pony?

"RUN along, Patsy," said Mother. "You'll be a big help to your Aunt Mary and Aunt Unity. Even if you are a little girl you can tell Henry and Sam and Joe what to do. They'll be too excited to remember to wait on people. You'll have to remind them. Have Henry get the younger servants to keep fires going outdoors for the barbecue. Sally and Susie must get Daisy-Chain and Lollie from the milkhouse to help them with the cooking. Mammy Tuck will take care of me."

Patsy ran along. The first person she saw in the yard was Captain George from the ship. He tossed her in the air and then danced a jig with her.

"I know something that's on the boat down there for Miss Dandridge," he shouted.

"When can I see it?" begged Patsy, hugging herself to keep from dancing up and down. Then she remembered her manners. Captain George hadn't had any good home cooking for months and months. He'd be hungry for good Virginia ham and corn bread and eggs and bacon and pie and the good things the Dandridges always had on the table.

"Of course you must have breakfast first," she said, though she didn't see how she was going to wait.

Henry had to go around the house twice, ringing the dinner bell, before he could get all the guests to come in to the table. Even Aunt Mary was late. She said she had seen ships come and go all her life in London, but she had never seen anything like this. "Everything means so much more here."

As soon as breakfast was over, the word went around that the Captain was going to get Patsy's present off the boat first.

Patsy couldn't wait any longer. "Is it something big?" she asked.

"Yes, sir, it's a pretty big package," teased the Captain.

"Package?" asked Patty.

"It's in a big box," said the Captain.

"A big box! Is it dead?" Patsy's heart seemed to stop beating.

"I don't think it ever was alive," chuckled the Captain, "but I'll wager you bring it to life one of these days."

By this time Patsy didn't know what to think. She had a sinking feeling, though, that she and the Captain weren't thinking of the same thing. What could it be that was dead and she could bring to life? She was so disappointed that it wasn't a pony she didn't care much what it was.

No one seemed to notice that she was unhappy. Men were swinging a big box over the side of the ship with a crane. They loaded it onto an oxcart. Now it came up the slope. Everybody crowded around.

"Where's Mr. Dandridge?" called the Cap-

tain. "Do you want us to open it here, or shall we take it into the house first?" he asked Father. Patsy saw that Father didn't know what to think either. "What is it?" he asked the Captain.

Captain George's mouth dropped open. "I thought you knew," he said. He called for two men to break open the box. "Be careful, now. Don't scratch it. Handle it gently."

In spite of herself Patsy began to get excited. What could this be that mustn't be scratched? It was dead, too. The cousins were as curious as she was. The men had trouble working the boards loose because there were so many people in the way. When the thing was finally opened Patsy knew no more than she did in the first place. It just looked like a polished wooden box that had caved in.

"It's broken, isn't it?" she asked.

"No, no, it just has to be set up," said Captain George, who seemed to know everything.

The minute they lifted it out of the crate and set it on the porch Cousin Martha let out a glad cry. "It's a spinet, the prettiest, loveliest spinet I have ever seen! Oh, Patsy, you're the luckiest girl in the world. I've wanted a spinet all my life, and this is much the finest one I've ever seen. Oh, will you let me play it?"

"Yes, indeed," said Patsy unhappily. "You may take it home with you and play it all you like."

Cousin Martha hugged her. "I couldn't do that," she laughed. "I'd certainly love to, though. Why, what's the matter, Patsy? You don't seem pleased at all."

Patsy couldn't keep back her tears. "I wanted a pony," she sobbed. "I thought it was a pony. You said I could bring it to life," she said to Captain George.

"I thought you could play a lively tune on it," said the Captain. "That would bring it to life, wouldn't it?" He wanted to make Patsy laugh, but she was too disappointed.

"Isn't it just a shame that it wasn't for Martha instead of Patsy?" said Aunt Unity. "John, I thought you were getting a pony for Patsy."

"So did I," said Father.

Just then Aunt Mary came out on the porch. She hadn't heard all that was going on.

"Why, how did you happen to uncrate the spinet here?" she asked in amazement.

"What do you mean, madam?" asked the Captain.

"Isn't that the spinet I sent for?" asked Aunt Mary. "Of course it is. I'd recognize my own spinet anywhere."

"Your spinet?" asked Father.

"Yes, I sent for it to give it to Martha for a wedding present."

Then they all burst out laughing. They had forgotten there were *two* Martha Dandridges.

"Then where's my pony?" asked Patsy.

"It's on the other ship," said Captain George. "It will be here before the day is old. We were never out of sight of each other. I just got into the river channel first."

"Since the spinet is here, suppose we set it up. Maybe Martha will play us a tune, and we'll all sing," said Father.

That was what they did, and there wasn't a happier voice in the crowd than Patsy's.

Boom! The other ship had come into the river. Soon it rounded the island. The first person at the landing was Patsy. Uncle William signaled the Captain to lift Patsy's pony over the side.

Mr. Smith looked the pony over. "It's the finest pony that ever set four feet on this shore," he said, "and look at him roll in the grass!"

"He knows he is home," said Patsy.

Riding Like a Flash

"Look out! Here comes Miss Patsy," cried old Henry. Sally and Susie were just going across the kitchen court with steaming dishes for the dinner table. They scooted when Henry called out. They had barely reached the doorway when Patsy and her pony flashed by.

"It's got so no place is safe around here any more," said Henry. "That little Miss Patsy and her pony go everywhere. First thing you know you hear hoofbeats and then—swoosh! Up and over you they come. Then they're gone before you can say 'Scat'!"

A year had passed since Patsy got her pony.

No one could have guessed that this was the same little girl who sat so patiently and watched her brothers ride. Mr. Smith couldn't believe his own eyes. She still looked the same, tiny and dainty, but she had changed decidedly.

"She's as quiet as a mouse in the house, but let her get on that pony and she's like a whirlwind."

Patsy's pony seemed to like to go as much as she did. And it was a good thing. They went everywhere and raced every other pony for miles around. No one could beat them.

"Miss Patsy will be ready to ride in the fox hunts this fall," Mr. Smith told her father. "I've never had a young lady learn to ride and jump and race a horse as quickly as she has."

Father was as proud as he could be. He and Mr. Smith had forgotten those weeks and weeks that Patsy had listened to Mr. Smith's lessons. But Patsy hadn't forgotten. It seemed to her that she had always known how to ride.

Patsy had learned more than riding this past year. Her mother had seen to that. "It's important that you know how to ride," she had said, "but there's a great deal more to managing a plantation than that. You do very well with your sewing now. You must learn to cook also."

"I won't need to know how to cook, Mother," said Patsy. "Mammy Tuck is teaching Lucy, and when I grow up I'll have Lucy do my cooking for me."

"What if something happened to Lucy?" asked Mother.

"Nothing's going to happen to her," said Patsy calmly. "I won't let it. I'll take good care of her."

"You can't always keep things from happening," Mother said. "What would you do if Lucy was sick?"

"I'd get somebody else who was a good cook."

"Where would you get her?"

"I'd go out and look for one."

"Where?"

"Where did you get Mammy Tuck? Surely it wouldn't be hard to find a good cook."

Mother laughed. "Mammy is a good cook now," she said. "But when she came here she was a young girl. She had never cooked before."

A surprised look came over Patsy's face.

"You're thinking about Mammy's gooseberry pies, I suppose."

"Yes," replied Patsy, "and all the other wonderful things Mammy cooks for us. I thought she *always* knew how to cook."

Mother laughed more heartily than ever. "Now you see how important it is to know how to cook yourself. So if you get a cook the way I got Mammy, you'd better learn how to cook, because I had to teach her everything."

Then Mother told Patsy how she had taught Mammy to clean kettles, to clean her kitchen, to clean the food, even before she taught her to cook.

"Mammy is smarter than many people, and she loved me so dearly that she learned quickly. You won't find a better cook anywhere. She'll make a good cook of Lucy, but it's safest to know how to do things yourself."

Patsy marched straight to the kitchen. She soon found that she had learned more than she knew, just by watching. She saw, too, that Mammy was mighty particular about clean kettles and clean hands. Mother had been a good teacher.

Patsy and Her Brother John

THE SUMMER was over. The crisp fall days had come. Every morning Sam built up fires in the great fireplaces. At noon it was hot outdoors, but by evening the fires felt good.

"We can look for our friends from Williamsburg any day now," said Mother. "The social season will be over. They'll be on their way home and will stop in for a few days."

That was the signal for Mammy Tuck. She took charge, issuing orders like a general.

"Bring down all the feather beds from the attic," she commanded Sam. "Set candles in the hall chandelier."

That chandelier was a beautiful one. It hung from the ceiling of the upstairs hall down the stair well to the first floor. It lighted both the upstairs and downstairs halls and both the wide stairways. The stairways were like those in the Governor's Palace at Williamsburg. Mammy Tuck was awfully proud of them.

"Your home is as elegant as anything you'll see when you go gallivanting as a young lady," she'd say to Patsy.

"Set new candles in all the wall brackets," Mammy ordered Sam now. "Polish the andirons."

The andirons already shone like gold, but Mammy enjoyed giving Sam orders.

"Henry," she went on, "bring out all the silver. Susie, get out the tablecloths. Nobody has finer linens than my Old Miss. We'll show 'em.

"Joe, get some of those field hands to roll up more logs for the fires. We'll need a whole forest of wood for the barbecues. And, Joe, have the blacksmith make some new spits."

Mammy gave orders day and night. By the time the first coaches rumbled through the forest and up the drive, she was ready for an army of visitors.

It looked as if she were going to have an army of them this year, too. "Everybody is coming," Patsy told Mammy Tuck. "Mother says Aunt Martha is bringing her little girl. That's my Cousin Molly. She's going to stay all year and we're going to have a school right here at this house.

"Guess who else is coming!" she went on.

"The Washingtons are coming, and the Henrys and the Wythes and the Macons. I know that," said Mammy Tuck.

Yes, Patsy knew that, too, but they weren't important to her. They were grownups. Father and Mother liked them. Father and Uncle William had fought in the same sea battles with Lawrence Washington. Patsy was talking about children.

"This is somebody who's coming from England to live with us."

Mammy Tuck gave up.

"It's Aunt Mary's son, William!" cried Patsy, pleased to be able to surprise Mammy.

Aunt Mary had changed. Now she loved Virginia. She liked the way people lived there. When she went home she decided to send her son William to live with his Uncle John, Patsy's father.

Every room, every nook and cranny in the house was full, and still visitors came. Aunt Unity had as many as Mother had. Nearly every family brought at least one servant besides their driver and footman, so the Negro servants had guests, too. All the cabins were full. There were parties going on all over the plantations. There were horse races during the day, barbecues in the evening, dances at night, and fox hunts at daybreak.

"Patsy, is it like this all the time here?" asked her new Cousin William. He had never known such fun, or eaten such good food. His head was whirling just from trying to see what was going on every place.

"Most of the time there isn't anyone here outside the family," Patsy told him. "I'm going to call you Will," she said, "because I already have a brother William and another Cousin William. The only times it's like this on the plantation are when the ship comes in and when we butcher."

Patsy herself was spinning like a top from one excitement to another. Here she had a new Cousin Will and a new Cousin Molly and her first fox hunt all at one time. The hunt was to be the next morning. Patsy had heard Mr. Smith tell Father she should go.

"Come see my pony, Molly," she said, proud to be able to show someone her own age around the place.

Molly didn't have a pony. She lived in Williamsburg and there wasn't much point in riding up and down its sandy streets. In fact, she couldn't see why Patsy was so excited. She didn't care at all about getting up before daybreak. But she wanted to be polite, so she went with Patsy to look at her pony.

When the pony saw Patsy coming in the gate, he trotted up to her. He tossed his head and kicked up his heels as if to say, "I know what we're going to be doing tomorrow."

Patsy always brought a bit of sugar in her pocket for the pony. He knew it. This morning when she didn't hand it to him at once, he pushed her in a friendly way. "Haven't you forgotten something?" he asked as plainly as if he had spoken.

140

"Look out!" cried Molly. "He's trying to bite you."

Molly ran for dear life to the gate. Patsy ran after her to explain. The pony thought it was a new game and ran, too. He reached the gate first. Poor Molly was so frightened her legs gave out from under her. She sprawled on the grass.

"Help! Help!" she cried. Mr. Smith came running, and so did Ned. Cousin Will and the boys ran up to her, too. They helped her up and lifted her onto the gatepost.

"It's all right," said Patsy. "I didn't know you were afraid of horses, Molly." She was a little ashamed of her cousin. "Here," she said to her, "the pony was trying to get the sugar I had for him. You give it to him. Then you'll see how gentle he is."

But Molly was afraid. "He might bite me."

"No, he won't. Hold the sugar out on the palm of your hand, like this."

But Molly wouldn't do it. Patsy gave her pet the sugar herself.

The two girls didn't enjoy each other much after this. Molly couldn't help feeling afraid. She had never been close to a pony or horse. At home she saw the horses only when they were already hitched to the coach. She wouldn't think of standing in front of them.

Patsy thought Molly was a " 'fraid cat." They were the same age, but Molly was bigger. Somehow or other, nothing was so much fun the rest of the day as it had been in the beginning.

At the barbecue the talk was all about the hunt set for the next morning. Cousin Will was happy because his uncle had given him a fine horse to ride. Will was older than Patsy. "Just watch me tomorrow," he said. "With this horse I'll clear every hurdle ahead of the field."

Will wasn't usually a show-off. He was so proud to be allowed to ride with the grownups, though, that he bragged in front of his little cousins. He had no idea that Patsy and her brothers could ride. It never occurred to him that Patsy would be allowed to ride in the big hunt. Children never took part in anything so important as this in England.

Uncle William came up while Will was talking. "Patsy will be riding in her first hunt in the morning," he said. "I hope you will keep an eye on her. You'd better stay behind the field a little way with her so that she won't be run down or make mistakes."

Will looked crushed. "If I have to play nursemaid I'd just as soon not go," he said, in his disappointment.

He didn't know that Patsy heard him, but she did. It spoiled the evening.

"Nothing's as much fun as I thought it would be," she said glumly. "But anyway I'll go on the fox hunt in the morning. Nobody can spoil that."

"Patsy," called Mother, "I've been looking everywhere for you. I must talk to you. I'm sorry, but I'm afraid you can't go with us in the morning. Since Molly doesn't ride and seems so unhappy, it would be rude of you to leave her. Besides, Will seems to think he would have to lag behind with you."

Patsy couldn't speak. She couldn't believe such a terrible thing as this could happen to anybody. She stood still and swallowed hard. She knew that her mother was right.

"If they weren't our guests, I wouldn't say a word," said Mother, "but I don't see anything else to do this time."

Someone called Mother then, and Patsy was left alone. She went around to the front porch, hoping there would be no one there. "I'll sit there where no one will see me," she thought. "Then I can cry."

But the porch was full of people. They were

singing and having a grand time. That made her feel worse than ever. She went to the back porch. That was full of folk talking about horses. The kitchen was full of Mammy's folk and extra kitchen help. Finally she slipped upstairs to the attic.

"Now I'll just cry till I'm dead," she said to

herself. She was about to begin when she heard a funny noise. It was a kind of squeak. Not quite a mouse's squeak. There! She heard it again.

She felt her way across the room and stumbled over something soft. It was a person—a boy. A little boy was up here crying with his head buried in one of the feather bags.

"Why, it's John!" cried Patsy. "John, what's the matter? I've never known you to cry before. What's happened? What is it, John? You can tell me. It's Patsy."

John didn't say anything for a while. He kept on making little choking sounds. Patsy waited, sitting in the dark beside him. The sounds of the singing and laughter below came in the windows.

Finally she said, "Is it about tomorrow? Aren't you to go either?"

John was to have gone on his first hunt in the morning, too. She felt fairly sure that was the trouble. All at once Patsy giggled. "I was coming up to cry about the same thing," she said. "Why aren't you allowed to go?"

John didn't answer. Then Patsy guessed what had happened. He had heard Mother tell her she shouldn't go. "You weren't going because I couldn't!" she cried. "Isn't that it?"

"It isn't fair," said John. "Every single time before this you've had to stay behind because you were too little. That old Molly!" he said fiercely.

Then Patsy laughed until she cried. She didn't feel sorry for herself at all any more. How could she when she had a brother like John?

"Don't you worry about me one minute, John. I don't mind missing the hunt at all. If you don't go tomorrow morning, I really *will* cry. You've got to go to show them how we can ride."

John sat up. Patsy didn't sound unhappy. "I'd like to show that Will up," he said. "He was hollering about being a nursemaid. You could beat

147

him and his big old horse any day. Let's get him to race tomorrow afternoon," he said eagerly.

Before they knew it they were laughing and talking, and bragging worse than Will ever had.

"It must be getting late," said Patsy suddenly. "You have to go to bed. You might fall asleep on your pony—and wouldn't that look fine!"

They had forgotten why they had gone to the attic. They went downstairs laughing and teasing each other.

Mother had been looking for them. When she heard their voices, a load was lifted from her heart. She knew they were all right.

Patsy Makes a Friend

PATSY piled the pillows over her head that night. She didn't want to hear the hunters start off the next morning. But when she fell asleep the pillows rolled off.

Before daylight she heard the excited whispers of the ladies in the halls and on the stairs. Outside there were laughter and gay voices. Down by the barn the dogs were barking. The grooms were saddling the horses by this time.

She wrapped a comfort around her and stood at the window. Bart and William heard her and came in and watched, too.

"There's John!" cried William. "He looks just

149

like any of the rest of them! Good old John! I hope his pony makes every jump. Next year maybe I'll be out there."

"I see Will," said Bart.

"Where?" asked Patsy.

"Over there by the walnut tree."

Will was standing by himself. He looked sad.

"Who's the tall man talking to Father?"

"That's Mr. Custis," said Patsy. "He's one of Mr. Washington's friends."

Just then Ned came down the lane leading Father's horse. The other grooms and stableboys began coming with the horses for their masters.

And then Patsy's heart came up into her throat —Joe was bringing her pony. He went all through the crowd, looking for Patsy.

"Your pony isn't going to like staying home," said William.

Finally Joe went to Mr. Dandridge. "I can't find Miss Patsy."

150

Will was feeling worse every minute. John had told him that Mother wouldn't let Patsy ride to the hunt. So Will went to Mr. Dandridge, too. He begged his uncle to send for Patsy. "I won't mind looking after her," he said.

Father was pleased with Will. So was Mr. Custis, for he had heard the whole story. "I'll wait for Miss Patsy with pleasure," he said. "The rest of you ride on. We'll catch up with you."

Father knew that Mr. Custis meant what he said. He sent Joe to ask Mother to call Patsy.

And at the same time Aunt Martha was asking Mother to do the same thing. "Molly won't even wake up till the hunt is over," she was saying. "It would be a shame to keep your Patsy out of the fun."

So Lucy fairly flew up to Patsy's room. "You boys scoot," she cried to William and Bart. "Miss Patsy's got to dress. She's going to ride."

The horn had sounded. The dogs were loosed.

The riders streamed out over the hillside. William and Bart watched anxiously.

"Patsy's going to be late," Bart worried.

"Mr. Custis will be cross," William said.

Mr. Custis wasn't cross. He had seen Patsy many times and he liked her. He thought she was too small to ride, though. He had never seen her on her pony.

When Patsy came out, so tiny and so pretty in her riding habit, he laughed aloud. "You're just a doll, only much prettier. We'll take a short cut and miss all the fences and hurdles and watch the fun from a distance."

Joe ran to her with her pony. She was up and away and motioning to Mr. Custis to come on before he had time to close his mouth.

"Look at them go," cried Bart. "Hurrah!"

"They'll catch the others. See if they don't!" yelled William.

Suddenly, just before they reached the first

ditch, Patsy wheeled her pony. "Oh, oh," thought Mr. Custis, "she's afraid."

But Patsy had remembered something. She raced her pony a little way back up the hill, and waved to the two little boys in the window. Then off she went again.

The boys waved madly. Kind little Patsy! She knew how it felt to have to stand and watch.

How the boys shouted when she cleared the first ditch! Without a pause she was off over the meadow like a streak. How they pounded each other on the back when Patsy and Mr. Custis caught up with the stragglers and passed them!

Mr. Custis had the ride of his life that morning. It was the beginning of a great friendship. Patsy liked this man who was gallant to a little girl on her first hunt. He admired the little girl who thought of her wistful brothers in the midst of her good times.

That was the first of many rides.

Let's Dance

THE HOUSE PARTY was over. The guests had gone. "Now it is high time to begin the lessons," said Mother.

The tutor thought so, too. The tutor's name was Mr. Treat.

"Lessons begin at seven in the morning," he said, "and last till breakfast time. We'll begin again at ten and stop at one. We'll study reading, spelling, and writing. The boys will have classes in figuring and geography while the girls embroider or weave as you see fit, Mrs. Dandridge. Boys and girls will have dancing together. The girls will learn also to play the spinet."

"You will have your classes in the north room," said Mother.

The classes began. Patsy wasn't interested. She was quiet and well behaved, and her manners were perfect, but she didn't do well in the studies. She couldn't wait to begin dancing.

"I already know how to dance," she whispered to Molly. "That will be fun because it's lively."

When the tutor told the children to line up for the dancing class, she skipped across the floor. She was as gay as a lark. She explained to Molly, "You'll like this. It's the Virginia Reel." She faced the line across the room and began to tap her foot and clap her hands.

A thunderous voice stopped her. "What are you doing?" roared the teacher. "What kind of jig step is that you're doing?"

"Don't you know it?" asked Patsy gaily. "Here, I'll show you." She took hold of the tutor's coattails and swung him around.

"Stop it! Stop it this minute!" bellowed Mr.
Treat. "We are not here to learn such pranks.
We are here to learn the minuet. Young lady,
this is a serious business. No more play."

"Dancing a business?" Patsy said to herself.
"That's silly."

Mr. Treat took his place at the head of the line.

157

"Now follow me and do exactly as I do," he commanded.

They followed him around and around the room. Patsy thought it was rather dull. She put just a little jig in the step. The tutor saw her in the mirror.

"Young lady," he roared again, "you look like a cork bobbing around on the water. Be graceful like your Cousin Molly. Watch her. Do as she does."

Patsy watched. She thought she was doing as Molly did. Mr. Treat thought not. The more he scolded, the worse Patsy bobbed. She thought the lesson would never end, but it finally did.

As soon as it was over she went to her mother. "I'm not going to dance any more," she said.

"Dancing is as important as riding, Patsy. I thought you enjoyed dancing."

"Mr. Treat says that what I do isn't dancing. It's jigging. Dancing isn't any fun at all and I

158

bob up and down and never could learn to do it anyway like Molly so I'm not going to try." Patsy said all that in one breath, because she was afraid she might cry if she took time to think.

"Patsy, when Molly first came you liked her, didn't you?"

"Yes," said Patsy.

"You don't like her so much now, do you? Do you know why?"

"Yes, because she is afraid of my pony and won't try to ride."

"You've found that dancing isn't what you thought it was. You're disappointed, so you won't try to like it. Molly is better than you at dancing; you are better than she is at riding. It seems too bad you can't help each other. You both ought to know dancing and riding."

Patsy leaned against her mother and watched her knit awhile. Then she went out of the room. Pretty soon Mother heard the two girls talking.

Molly was saying, "I'd love to try again. I've been so ashamed of the way I acted with your pony."

"And I'm ashamed of the way I bob up and down in the dance," said Patsy. "Oh, Molly, I'm glad we're friends again. We can have fun helping each other."

Mother Is in Earnest

MRS. DANDRIDGE and Patsy and Molly and Cousin Anna were going to see Cousin Martha Aylett. They were going on horseback. Funny big bundles of wool were slung over the backs of their saddles. Molly and Patsy were arguing about these with Mother.

"It's such a lot of work, carding this wool," they were saying. "We can just stop at Mr. Coomb's in the village and leave it with him."

"No," said Mother firmly. "I want you girls to card this wool yourselves. You must know how."

"We do know how," said Patsy. "We've watched our weaving women for hours."

161

Patsy and Molly were nearly young ladies now. Four years had passed since the two girls had their first dancing lesson together. They felt that they knew about all they needed to know. But Mother didn't agree with them.

"There's a great deal more to running a plantation than knowing how to dance and ride and

cook and sew. You must know how to manage," said Mother. "You will have to look after your own families and the workers' families. You have to know how to do just about everything that's done on a plantation. One of the most important things is knowing how to make clothes. Watching someone else do it isn't the same as doing it yourselves. You must do it over and over until you can't forget it."

"Please, Mother," said Patsy. "We'll do it because you tell us to, but really, there's no sense to it. The boats bring plenty of cloth from England now. I'll never have to weave."

"You think now you won't," said Mother. "That's just what I said to my mother when I was married. I was marrying a rich man, I said. I wouldn't need to know how to do things. There was plenty of money no matter what things cost. We didn't worry.

"Then one year there was a rot that spoiled

our tobacco. We lost the whole crop. Tobacco was money in those days, just as it is now.

" 'Never mind,' we told ourselves, 'next year's crop will make up for this year's.' But the next year there were terrible floods, and many cabins were washed away. The tobacco fields were under water. There was no money that year. We began to worry.

"The next year there was plenty of tobacco. We borrowed on it, and were happy again. Then one day before the tobacco was cut there was a hailstorm. It hailed as I never have seen it hail. The leaves were stripped off the tobacco plants. We were ruined."

"What did you do?" asked Cousin Anna.

"We went without things. We had no money for clothes or provisions. We were hungry. Our clothes were ragged.

"The next spring we sowed grass seed and raised sheep and cows. We began to manage.

'Even if the tobacco crop fails, we'll have enough food and wool to keep us comfortable from now on,' we promised ourselves.

"Every year since then, Mr. Dandridge has had enough money to take care of the people on the plantation. Ever since then we have made all our everyday clothes. We have had someone else make only our best silk and satin clothes.

"England is too far away. The women in this country must know how to feed and clothe their families with or without England's help."

Mother was very much in earnest. The girls felt the cloth in their dresses. Any girl would be proud to have made such fine, soft cloth.

"I'm not going to complain any more, Mother," said Patsy. "And I'm going to learn to make cloth as fine as this."

"When you have learned to do that," said Mother, "you will be ready to become the mistress of your own plantation."

Off to Williamsburg

THE COACH was at the door. The trunks were already strapped in place. Mother and Father were setting off for Williamsburg again with Uncle William and Aunt Unity as usual.

It was spring. The daffodils and tulips and magnolias were in full bloom. Everything was just as it had been the year Patsy cried because the family went to Williamsburg without her. That had been nine years ago. This year Patsy's little sister Anna watched for Uncle William and Aunt Unity.

"I just got to see my little Patsy at her first Governor's ball," said Mammy Tuck to Mrs.

Dandridge. "I want to see the gentlemen's eyes pop out when they see her step out on the ballroom floor."

Mother laughed. "They're used to pretty girls, Mammy," she said. "Besides, Patsy is so small they won't see her over the heads of the other beauties there."

"Makes no difference," declared Mammy Tuck. "Nobody else has her style, or her looks, or has so many pretty dresses."

Patsy did have pretty dresses. The ball gowns were the last word in elegance. "Nobody need know you made these yourself, Miss Patsy," said Mammy Tuck. She was packing them carefully.

"I want people to know," said Patsy. "I'm proud of it. I'd like them to notice my coat and know that I made the cloth for it. I raised the lambs, and sheared the sheep, and carded the wool, and made the yarn, and made the dye, and dyed the yarn and wove it into cloth, and dressed it, and cut out the coat and stitched it, all with my own two hands!"

Mammy looked at Patsy's dainty little white hands. "Don't you dare tell anybody all that," she said. "Let 'em think you paid a thousand pounds of tobacco for it. They'll think it's twice as pretty."

Mother smiled.

"That's why I have to go to Williamsburg, Old Miss," said Mammy anxiously. "Miss Patsy mustn't make mistakes like telling people things like that."

So Mammy Tuck was going to Williamsburg, too.

It was the first time that Patsy had ever been to a town. Of course they went through New Kent on the way to St. Peter's Church every Sunday. But New Kent wasn't much bigger than the village on the plantation.

Williamsburg was twenty-two miles away. It

was not too far for a day's journey, but the road was bad. It went through a deep forest, and there were mudholes and swollen streams to pass.

They started out early in the morning. It was night when they reached Williamsburg. The street lanterns were lighted. Light shone from all the windows in the houses they passed by. To Patsy, it looked like fairyland.

"I had no idea it would be so exciting!" she said.

They went past one great big house where there were coaches and horses drawn up in lines. Ladies in satins and silks, gentlemen in satin coats and knee breeches were coming and going. Through the door came sounds of music and laughter.

Patsy's heart began to flutter. "Wouldn't it be fun to be invited to a party at that house?"

But then, of course, she wouldn't be. She was

169

just a country girl. These people belonged here
at the Governor's court. This was their home.

Patsy tried not to stare, but she couldn't take
her eyes away from the gay scene. A gentleman
came out on the front steps. From the way people bowed, the way the grooms grinned and the
servants scraped, she knew he must be a person

of importance. He turned toward her. By the light in the doorway she saw that it was Mr. Custis.

At the same moment he saw the Dandridge coach and called out. Ned pulled the horses to a stop.

"I've been watching for you," said Mr. Custis. He came to the coach window. "Colonel Dandridge and the others passed a few minutes ago and said you were coming. I thought Miss Patsy was coming——"

At that moment he saw Patsy.

"Good evening, Mr. Custis," said Patsy.

Poor Mr. Custis couldn't say a word. He had not been expecting a young lady. He had been thinking of Patsy as a little girl on a pony. Suddenly he found himself falling head over heels in love with her.

"Come in, won't you?" he said. "Meet my friends. Many of them you know already."

"It's been a long journey," said Mother. "I think it best that we go on tonight."

So they went on. They passed the Bruton Parish House.

"That is where my grandfather, your great-grandfather, preached," said Mother. "He was the first minister of this parish. There's the Governor's Palace."

Patsy would have guessed that without being told. It was as grand as any palace she had ever imagined. It was fairly ablaze with lights. And she would be going there only a few nights from this! Her heart began to pound again.

It didn't take long for word to get around that there was a new belle in town. Everywhere people were whispering, "They say Mr. Custis can't let Miss Patsy Dandridge out of sight."

That set the young ladies' tongues to wagging. "I've heard," said one who was a little jealous, "that she is just a drudge. She can sew and cook

172

and garden. I can't understand what a man of Mr. Custis' wealth sees in a farmer maid."

"They say she can make anything grow. Her garden is a show place. What a sight her hands must be!"

"Her arms are probably hard and lumpy with muscles."

"No doubt she's just an ox of a woman. Her cousin Molly has told me there isn't anything she can't do. Molly simply worships her."

"If Molly Macon likes her, we'll all like her," said Betty Claiborne.

"We'll soon see," they said.

When they met Patsy, they knew that Molly had been right.

"She's like a princess," they said.

"She's as kind as she is pretty, too," said one young lady named Evelyn. "My maid was sick and Patsy stayed home and helped me take care of her and missed the tea at the Carys'."

"She let me wear her lovely new bonnet. 'I'm not going to the Carys', so won't you please wear it?' she said. There never was anyone more generous," said Betty.

"She's more fun than anybody, too. No matter what you're doing it's better if Patsy's in on it. If you're sad she cheers you up. If you're glad she makes you still happier."

"If she dances as well as she does everything else she'll be the favorite at the Governor's ball tomorrow night," they declared.

At the Grand Ball

IN EVERY HOUSE the next evening people were dressing for the grand ball. They had begun in the middle of the afternoon. Hairdressers went from family to family. Dressmakers hurried from place to place. They were making last-minute changes in ruffles or hoop skirts. The jeweler didn't have a single trinket left. The hosier, the cobbler, and the tailor were worn out. They had been up night after night getting their customers fitted.

As the hour of the opening drew near, there wasn't anyone who wasn't atwitter. One person, though, topped them all. In the whole town of

Williamsburg there wasn't anyone more excited than Mammy Tuck.

"Now, honey," she said to Patsy, "turn around once more, real slow, so I can see if any little thing is out of place."

Patsy turned slowly. Mammy Tuck finally said she was just right, and she was. Patsy wasn't too tall or too short. She wasn't too thin or too fat. Her eyes were big and round and hazel-colored. Her hair was dark brown with a little curl in it. Her complexion was like peaches and cream. She fairly sparkled tonight, she was so happy. Mammy Tuck couldn't find a single flaw.

The footmen began to announce the arrival of coaches for the ladies. The Dandridge coach was at the door.

Molly and Patsy, Mother and Aunt Unity and Aunt Martha were all going to the Governor's Palace together. Mammy Tuck went with them.

She had to see that everything about their dresses was right before the ladies started to dance. There were other coaches waiting behind the Dandridge coach. The gentlemen rode on horseback beside their ladies' coaches.

When Patsy came through the doorway, there was a crowd of riders to surround the coach. Molly squeezed Patsy's hand. "Patsy, you're already the belle of the ball!"

In the Palace the fiddlers were tuning up. The ladies and gentlemen were coming into the ballroom to be presented to the Governor. The light from hundreds of candles in the chandeliers and wall brackets set the ladies' jewels to twinkling. The room was a rainbow of color.

Mammy Tuck stood in the balcony and looked down on it. Other ladies' maids stood near Mammy. Each was picking out her mistress. Each thought hers would be the Governor's

choice for the most graceful dancer. Mother had told Mammy there were so many beauties that Patsy would hardly be noticed. But Mammy wasn't worried. She knew who was the prettiest young lady there.

When the fiddlers began to play, Mammy wasn't at all surprised to see the Governor take Miss Patsy away from Mr. Custis. Not only that, Mr. Custis had a hard time to get near Miss Patsy again that whole evening. Everybody wanted to dance with her.

All the rest of the time the Dandridges were in Williamsburg Mr. Custis couldn't get any time alone with her. So when the Dandridges went home he escorted them. Others went, too, but it was easy to see that he was the favorite.

Not two years later Patsy Dandridge became Mrs. Daniel Parke Custis.

Mistress of
Mount Vernon

EVERYBODY had thought that Mr. Custis and Patsy would live happily ever after. For a while they did live happily. They had four children and everything that money could buy. They had the big house in Williamsburg and an estate in the country and hundreds of servants.

Patsy seemed to have everything that anyone could wish for. But sorrows came to spoil her happiness. Two of her children died, and soon afterward Mr. Custis died, too.

Poor little Patsy! She didn't think she could ever smile again, but there was work to do. She had to manage the Custis estate.

People said, "She'll never be able to run that big place. It will be hard to manage so many servants. Field hands won't take orders from a woman. And the Indians may make trouble for her. No woman can live alone."

But people didn't know Patsy. They didn't know how carefully Mrs. Dandridge had trained her.

All the servants worked hard. "We want to help Miss Patsy," they said.

The Indians were Patsy's friends, too. They didn't bother anyone who trusted them.

Patsy managed, but she wasn't happy. She was lonely. She worried about her little boy and girl. "Children need a father," she said, "especially rich children. Everyone spoils them, and I'm too easy on them."

Her friends begged her to come back to the balls and court life of Williamsburg. "No one can give a ball and entertain as you can, Patsy.

The parties are never so gay as when you are there."

Patsy couldn't go to the balls. Her heart was too sad.

One day she was visiting her friends, the Chamberlynes. Their home was on the York River, not far from the ferry. They could see the boats from their front windows. This day Mr. Chamberlyne saw a tall soldier and his servant and their horses being ferried across the river.

"Why, I believe that's George Washington," he said. He hurried to invite him to dinner.

Patsy went to the window. She wanted to meet George Washington. Of course she knew who he was. There wasn't anyone in Virginia who didn't. Everyone had heard how he had two horses shot out from under him in the French and Indian Wars. He had had four bullet holes through his coat. Now he was commander in chief of the armies of Virginia.

But Patsy wanted to know more about him than that. What was he really like? Patsy and his mother, Mrs. Mary Washington, were good friends. Mrs. Washington had told her that George was more of a farmer than a soldier. He loved to ride over his plantation at Mount Vernon, and plant things and watch them grow.

Just then Mr. Chamberlyne brought George Washington to Patsy. The tall soldier looked at pretty little Patsy in her silk dress with the hoop skirt. He liked her silly high-heeled satin slippers, and her saucy bows and ribbons.

"I know about you," he said. "My mother told me. She said you dress as if the only things you care about are balls and parties, but that you're really a farmer's daughter in disguise!"

How Patsy laughed at that! It was the first time the Chamberlynes had heard her laugh since Mr. Custis died.

George and Patsy became fast friends. Patsy

knew she could trust this man. Her two children adored him.

Several months after that first meeting Patsy and George were married. The wedding was at her home on the Pamunkey River.

Once more the coach stood at the back door. The driver was on his post, the footman was at the door. Patsy was going to Williamsburg again. This time the family was staying behind—even Mammy Tuck. But many of the wedding guests were going to escort the bride and groom on their way. Even the Governor of Virginia would ride with them.

No one who saw Patsy that day ever forgot how lovely she looked. Her dress was too pretty for words. The petticoat was of quilted white satin. The overskirt was made of white corded silk embroidered with silver thread. In her hair she wore pearls. Her earrings were set with diamonds and pearls and so were her bracelets and necklace. On her feet she wore the high-heeled satin slippers George liked so well.

"You always were the prettiest little girl in Virginia," said Mammy Tuck, when Patsy came out to the coach. "Today you are the most beautiful woman in the world." Of course Mammy Tuck was prejudiced.

Then the driver cracked his whip—the coach was off. In the last glimpse Patsy had of her old home she saw Mammy pull off her shoe and throw it after the coach, for good luck.

As soon as the court season at Williamsburg was over, Patsy and George went to live at George's home, Mount Vernon, on the Potomac River. It reminded Patsy of her father's plantation. She and George loved it. They were as happy as the day is long.

It didn't seem possible that anything sad could happen to Patsy again. George wouldn't let it happen! But it did.

The First
"First Lady"

THERE WAS WAR. The colonists were fighting for their independence. George Washington had been chosen commander in chief of all the armies for the American cause.

All the ports were closed. No ships were coming in or going out for the colonists. That meant that no food, clothing, guns, or supplies for the armies, were coming in from the outside.

Mrs. Dandridge had once said, "The women of this country must know how to do things."

Patsy remembered that now. While she had been living in Williamsburg all she had needed to know was how to be a fashionable lady.

Now she needed to know how to do things—to preserve foods, raise crops and livestock, and above all, how to weave. Patsy went to visit George Washington in his winter camp at Valley Forge. She had seen the suffering of the soldiers. They had hardly enough clothes to cover themselves. Many had no shoes. She had seen the bloody tracks of their frozen feet in the snow.

She had bandaged wounds, and fed the starving men from stores of food she brought from Mount Vernon. She had knelt beside the dying and given comfort to their families.

Patsy's hands were never idle. She wrote to her brothers and sisters, to her friends in Williamsburg, "Get out your spinning wheels. Start your looms again. Spin! Weave! Brave men are freezing to death for want of good warm clothing."

Patsy herself had fifteen spinning wheels going day and night at Mount Vernon. All of them

were spinning wool to make cloth for the soldiers' clothes.

She had no use in those days for silk or satin dresses. She wore a gray homespun dress, with a gingham apron.

Every morning she set out, followed by Lucy carrying a huge basket filled with soups and jellies for the soldiers. Their faces always lighted up at the sight of this plainly dressed little woman as she went about her rounds of mercy.

The war lasted seven years. Every summer Patsy went back to Mount Vernon to raise food and get supplies ready for the winter.

During the winter months she stayed at her husband's headquarters. In the evening she would sit before the fire, her back as straight as when she was a little girl, knitting socks for the soldiers. As she worked she talked to George. She told him funny little happenings at home, at Mount Vernon. She told him what the grandchildren were saying and doing. She chatted as if she hadn't a care in the world. It gave him courage and strength just to see and hear her.

The war finally ended. The colonies became the United States of America. Now the women brought out their bright-colored dresses, their ribbons and satins and velvets, their jewels and dainty slippers.

George and Martha Washington wished to go to Mount Vernon to live, but they couldn't. He was elected President of the new nation. She became the first "First Lady" of the land.

At the Inaugural Ball in New York they stood side by side to receive the guests. There were representatives of foreign nations present. There were generals and statesmen, men of wealth and influence, ladies from foreign courts and ladies from all parts of the new nation.

They all looked distinguished, the new President and his wife most of all. He was dressed in a handsome black broadcloth coat and knee breeches and a white shirt with ruffles and lace at the cuffs. He was proud to say that all the materials had come from his own plantation of Mount Vernon. He wore a dress sword, too, sheathed in white leather.

Martha Washington looked the part of the President's wife in her brocaded silk gown, with jewels in her hair. It would have been hard to guess the sorrow that was in her heart. Her daughter had died and her son had been killed the last day of the war. But, as always, she put aside her own grief to think of the happiness of others. So she stood there, smiling and gracious, at the side of her honored husband.

Worldly people thought, "How fortunate it is that the President's wife is a woman of charm and dignity."

Her countrymen thought, "Martha Washington shows the world a new kind of lady, the

American woman. She is just as fine whether she is kneeling in the snow beside the wounded or standing beside her husband in the highest place in the land."

Her husband thought, "How beautiful she is; how kind and cheerful and thoughtful—dear little Patsy!"

George Washington was President for eight years. At last, in 1797, he and Martha went back to Mount Vernon to live. They were very happy to be on the plantation again.

There, during the next few years, the first President and the first "First Lady" spent some of the best days of their lives.